Frum
SCHOOLDAYS
to
THE ARCTIC CIRCLE
and Beyond

*"From a boy still wet behind the ears
to a man who was destined to be a Hull trawlerman
and, given the chance, would do it all over again"*

KENNETH SHAKESBY

Grosvenor House
Publishing Limited

This book is published by
Grosvenor House Publishing Ltd
Link House
140 The Broadway, Tolworth, Surrey, KT6 7HT.
www.grosvenorhousepublishing.co.uk

A CIP record for this book
is available from the British Library

Printed and bound in the United Kingdom by
Lightning Source UK Ltd., Milton Keynes

ISBN 978-1-78623-437-7

To my lovely wife, Jean, and my family,
who encouraged me to write this book.

I would like to thank everyone who
helped me put my memoir on paper.

I hope that the people who read my book will truly enjoy it.
I have been writing it for a number of years, because the
events which happened will stay in my mind forever. I remember
it like it was yesterday. I will never forget the men I sailed with
on the Hull trawlers, or the thousands who sailed out of the
Hull fish dock and never returned.

I am very proud to say I was part of Hull's deep-sea trawling fleet.

The Hull trawler, 'Portia', where I started as mate in August 1973. I was so proud of the crews who worked with me during my period on board the 'Portia'.

Contents

Chapter 1

THE BEGINNING AND BEYOND

The story begins before I left school. I was about nine years old and at primary school, which was situated off Hessle Road, down a street called Somerset Street (hence the name Somerset Primary School) and my house was on Carlton Street, which was at the outer end of Hessle Road. I know this will sound strange to you, but please bear with me, as this is the beginning. Where I lived, on Carlton Street, at the bottom of our arch, were stables where several horses were kept. Please remember, in the fishing industry, the horse was one of the most valuable modes of work power. These horses pulled trailers full of fish for potential buyers.

In my childlike curiosity, I would go to the horses each day, and I got friendly with the 'keeper'. I would help him clean the horses out and feed them.

Eventually, I got really involved, and at the age of 10, it was a massive event for me. The horses were normally driven by the same driver, so I became good friends with him. One of the strangest things is that, later in life, I became very friendly with the son of the owner of the horses, as they belonged to a haulage company.

Now back to the beginning. . . this was part of my daily life. I used to leave school, I think at 3.30pm and wait. What was I waiting for? Banker, my favourite horse, would have finished on the docks.

As soon as the driver arrived, I would jump up next to him and he would pass me the reins. I would drive Banker all the way down Woodcock Street, then up Hawthorne Avenue onto Hessle Road, and then down Carlton Street to the stable.

1

I felt good and really proud of what I was doing, and this event continued for two years, before my mam decided to move house, from Carlton Street to Conway Street, which was close to West Dock Avenue.

From there, I went to Boulevard High School which, of course, was on a road called Boulevard. It was not too far for me to walk, and that is where I stayed until December 1963, when I was 15 years old. It was good, as a few weeks prior to leaving school, the headmaster told all the boys (it was an all-boys school) that we could go out and look for work. So, of course, a few of us went down to the fish dock, looking for work on the trawlers. I felt that was where I wanted to be.

Hopefully, all the seafarers and 'land lubbers' will find some enjoyment and truths in this book. There will be good things and not so good things. I will enter this small period of my life before I went to sea, as it is relative to the sea.

My father was a fisherman and, as I write my book, he is with me (in spirit), helping me to put this story onto paper.

My dad was employed with St Andrews Steam Fishing Company at the time. He was mate, and his job was to sail on the 'purse seiner' vessel. I appreciate that a lot of people will know what a 'purse seiner' fishing vessel does with its nets. For the people who do not, it is a fishing vessel which puts its nets down and, when the time comes, a smaller boat is used to take one end and secure it to the other, so it forms a circle and no fish can escape. Then, the larger vessel hauls the net on board.

Like I said, my dad was to sail mate (or second hand; the position was the same). He and other officers were to sail the 'Asoukow'. There was also a sister vessel called the 'Amanzule'. The job was to sail to West Africa and work off Ghana, fishing for tuna. Their home port would be Tema, Ghana.

So, the ships set sail. I was just a young boy of 13 and, like all kids my age, was mainly doing paper jobs; delivering the local newspapers. Time was passing by and my dad was still fishing in Ghana, so I believed all was OK. I used to spend my hard-earned paper money at the local roller-skating rink, which I enjoyed very much. You will see, later in the book, that I sailed with a skipper called Kenny Rose, who lived very close to our house. He had a small son, also called Kenneth, and I used to take him around with me.

So, after my dad had completed seven consecutive months on the ship, he and others decided to come home, as enough was enough. Well, my dad comes home and, of course, he tells us all his sea stories. We were all amazed, and then my dad decided to return to the Hull trawlers. He went with a company called J.W. Marr.

One day, I went to town for something, and little Kenneth came with me, for a day out. I remember my dad was at home. Anyway, we ventured to town and what a surprise I got as we were walking along. . . you could see the ships from the main street, and I saw the two ships my dad was with in Ghana! I said to Kenneth, "Let's go and have a look!"

We climbed on board and, please remember, at this time, I think I was about 13-14 years old and little Kenneth would have been five or six. The ship was in semi-darkness and we were shouting "Hello!" and eventually someone came. He was a crew member, a man from Ghana, so Kenneth and I were taken aback by his speech, as he could not really speak English, and he was shouting, "What you want? Why you here?"

Anyhow, I managed to spit out that my father was the chief officer on the ship before. The man asked me my father's name and, of course, I managed to get his name out. Our family name, Shakesby, did not mean anything to the man, but as soon as I said "Mr Walter," (which was how the African crew addressed their officers) everything stopped and all went quiet. He just repeated my dad's name very quietly; "Mr Walter, Mr Walter!" Then everything was

3

OK and he was such a nice man! He asked me if it would be possible to meet my dad and I said, "Why not?"

So, the crewman, Kenneth and I jumped on the trolley bus (No 70!) down to Hessle Road to a pub called Rayners. I told the crewman that my dad would be in the bar, but he said he did not drink or go in bars, so I ended up sneaking in, seeing my dad and taking him outside to meet the man.

The crewman was so excited when he saw my dad, but still he refused the invitation to go into the pub, so they agreed that he would return to his ship in the town, then, in the evening, pop to our house (my dad explained where it was) with one or two other crew members. So, the man went back to his ship, my dad went back into the pub and Kenneth and myself went back home. All was good, (or so I thought!)

That evening, I was getting washed and changed to go to our local youth club. It was about 7pm and my family had finished tea and were just relaxing, watching television and reading the local newspaper. Then there was a knock on the back door and I opened it and all I saw were a pair of eyes and white teeth, then more gathered around and my eyes adjusted to the dark night, and I realised that they were the crew members, (there were maybe six or eight of them).

I immediately shouted for my dad, then he invited them in. I had three sisters, who would have been aged between 15 and 20, so they were a bit embarrassed. Anyhow, the crewmen came in and sat down to watch television (I do believe that they had never seen a television before).

My mother came through from one of the other rooms and when she saw the crewmen, she screamed (as no one had bothered to tell her they were coming) then ran back through the house, grabbed her coat and was out on the street as fast as lightning.

The crewmen stayed for about 30 minutes, then they decided to leave. They were very respectful and gracious. The next problem was. . . where was our mam? Anyhow, we looked up and down the road and eventually walked to our auntie's. Our mam was there, and we sat and had a cup of tea. My mam saw the funny side of the situation and came home with us, and all was ok. Even though this happened all those years ago, I still remember it like it was only last week.

It all started in July of 1961, when I was a young lad of 13 years, approaching my 14th birthday in the coming October. With my father working as mate/bosun on Hull's deep-sea fishing fleet, it was, of course, in my blood that I would eventually follow the same path. At this time, my best pal, Kenny Roberts, had just started on the trawlers. I would sleep at his mam and dad's house and wake up early to set him away to sea. I just could not wait until I had left school and it was my time to go to sea.

I remember one time, when I was at this ripe old age of around 13 years, (this was before I did my 'pleasure trip'); my father was sailing for a company called Hendricksons and he was bosun on the 'Victrix'. It was not a new ship, but they were doing OK financially. On this particular trip, the ship had docked at Grimsby, on the other side of the River Humber. What happens is that the crew come home once the ship is secured and everything is safe on board, then the following day, when the ship has landed its catch, a 'skeleton' crew take the ship back to Hull.

The 'next day' was a Sunday, when my father and the crew would go around to bring the ship back to Hull. So, on the Saturday evening, I asked my father if I could go with him, and he said, "Yes, son." So, I went to bed on the Saturday evening, excited and looking forward to the morning. My dad said he would leave about 7:30am.

I woke up suddenly the next morning and looked at the clock. It said 8:30am! I jumped out of bed and ran downstairs.

My mam was sitting there and I asked where dad was, and she said he had gone! I felt gutted that he had left me behind. I asked

Mam, "Why didn't he wake me?" and Mam said he did not want to disturb me. I felt so angry as I had been really looking forward to this. I had never actually sailed down the River Humber on a trawler before and felt bad that my dad had left me.

I made my mind up and asked Mam to give me the bus fare to get to town, as the route my dad would take was to town, down to the ferry terminal, across the River Humber on a ferry to New Holland, then from there, by train, to Grimsby. No more to be said; I was out of my house like a flash and got to the nearest bus stop. No buses for at least 15-20 minutes! There was no way I was going to wait; I could picture my dad on the ferry, waiting to sail.

I ran all the way to the ferry wharf, which is still called Minerva Pier, in town. I saw the ferry just about to pull away from the berth, so I ran down the ramp. I could hear people shouting after me and then I saw my dad. He came and got me and gave my fare to the ticket person. So I was on board and underway to Grimsby to pick up the 'Victrix' and bring it back to Hull!

We arrived at New Holland (Lincolnshire) and got the train to Grimsby. We reached the 'Victrix' in the late morning and the crew went about their duties to make sure all was working before we left Grimsby.

I felt really good, going down the River Humber. I also went onto the bridge and the Skipper let me steer the ship for a while. It was good fun!

Then we arrived at St Andrews Dock in Hull and went through the lock pits and into the dock, tied up the ship alongside the quay and Dad and I got a taxi and went home. I really was glad I had decided to run to town, or I would have missed the ferry! My dad said, "Well, son, you are determined to go to sea!"

Why this little 'trip' from Grimsby to Hull meant so much to me was because, in the past, my sister and I would go and meet my dad's ship at the entrance to the dock, then we would climb on board and stay until they secured the ship to the dock, so the ship would already be in position for discharging her catch the following day.

Going through the docks was good for me, and also, the next morning, my dad and I would walk down to the fish dock and Dad would collect his 'fry'; the certain amount of fish each crew member was allowed. Then, we would walk back home again, and I would stop at the hotcake shop and get some for our breakfast. I can smell those hotcakes, even now. I really do believe they were the good old days.

When we got back to the house, my dad would fillet the haddock and we would keep some for our family and give some to our friends and neighbours. I would carry on that tradition in my 'trawling life'. I would do exactly as my father before me did. Even to this day, I will get some 'fresh fish' from the wet fish shop (always haddock) and cook it for our tea.

Ships had always been in my thoughts, and it seemed a good, adventurous life, so at the ripe old age of 13 years and eight months, I decided I would like to do a 'pleasure trip' on the deep-sea trawlers. Today, I believe we would refer to it as a work opportunity scheme. The system was that if you were interested, you would meet with the owners of the company you would like to go with, and if all agreed, you would sail in one of their vessels.

At the time, I was very fortunate as, down our street, we had Ken Rose, the trawler skipper, and when I spoke to him regarding the 'pleasure trip,' he instantly agreed to take me with him on his next voyage. So, we decided to meet with the company officials to get permission for me to go on the skipper's next trip. The company's name was Lord Line; a very large and prosperous company.

The meeting turned out to be a disaster, as after all had been discussed and it was just a matter of preparation, one man asked me, "How old are you?" I immediately answered, in a schoolboy manner, "Fourteen years old this coming October!" I thought I had called him bad words, as the look on his face was really soul-destroying. He replied, "There is absolutely no way you can do the trip this year, as the official age is fourteen and not a day under."

I felt like someone had just taken my world away. I was so upset, I just ran out of the office, shouting, "You are all bastards! No one wants to let me go!" (Please remember, these words were from a schoolboy who, at that time, did not even know what the word 'bastard' meant!)

I ran home as fast as my legs could carry me and was so upset that when I got there, I just could not get the words out to my mother and father.

When, eventually, my parents managed to console me, and I quietened down, I explained what had happened and then there were a knock on the door. It was the skipper from down our street. Straight away, I apologised for my behaviour, and he said, "Don't worry," as that had been his opinion too, so that made me laugh a little.

For the next few hours, my parents, the skipper and myself discussed the situation to see if there was any way around the problem. The skipper came up with a very good solution and it was this: I would go on board the trawler when she was ready for sailing (this event was normal, as all sons set their fathers off to sea, so it would not be anything out of the ordinary). I would then go to the forward accommodation of the ship and sit down. Then, when the company's runner came on board for last minute checks, I would just say, "I will leave in a moment, when I have said my farewells" etc.

'Lord Essendon', my first trip on a trawler as a pleasurer.
I was 13 years and eight months old. (Skipper Kenny Rose).

This sounded like a good plan, so on the sailing day, I bade farewell to my parents and went marching on board the 'Lord Essendon' like an old sea dog. To say the least, she was old! I went down below to the focsle (forecastle) and there were some crewmen and their sons sitting there, chatting and exchanging sad looks, having a farewell drink, as was the tradition in those days. I plopped my kitbag down (I had three weeks' worth of warm clothing inside, as my father had advised me to do) and just sat there, waiting for the time to pass.

The company's runner (Jack Waller) was the man who would make sure that all crew members were on board and all the 'visitors' had left. He bellowed, "All passengers and stowaways off!" so I knew I was just about there for departure. I gave the runner a little boy's smile and said I would just say ta-ra to my father (who was sitting at home!) as he did not know to whom I belonged.

The crew members started to get into their working clothes, so I hid out of sight for a while. The next moment, I was hearing "Leggo forward" and "Leggo aft" (which, of course, means let go of the mooring ropes), then I heard the faint throbbing of the engines and a couple of light nudges and I knew we were off and clear of the dock.

We were then into the River Humber. In my hiding place, I could see out of a small porthole.

About three hours later, I felt the ship moving about more, so decided I would venture out of my hiding place and see what was in store for me. At that moment, one of the crew members, who was spare hand (another name for deck hand) appeared and I fell into him. I don't remember who was more shocked; me or him!

He said to me, "Come on, young 'un, I'm taking you to the old man!" (Which old man, I did not know, but I found out later that he meant the skipper!) I was taken to the wheelhouse (called bridge for seafarers) and the skipper was there, as well as the mate, but the biggest shock of all was that one of my school friends, who lived nearby, was there with his father!

I was flabbergasted and then the story came out; my friend, Tony Martin, whose father was a spare hand on the trawler, had also decided to stow away! We just looked at each other and gave a boyish nod. This is when I kicked off my school shoes and put on my thigh boots (rubber wellington boots which go all the way up to the thigh).

Then the skipper started to talk and, of course, he knew I would be there, but hadn't known that my friend Tony would be doing the same. Not only that, but the skipper then told us that, on board, were two more pleasurers from the Royal Air Force! We had ended up with four persons (two stowaways and two legal), but it was all out in the open and I felt better. The skipper said he should return to discharge my friend and I but decided we could stay. Then he read the riot act out to us all.

Things would get worse as time passed by, believe me, but now, as we chugged steadily up towards Iceland on a nice summer's day, life did not seem too bad!

We were steaming up north to the Icelandic fishing grounds and in the North Sea, there was a lazy summer swell, which just made our trawler do lazy rolls. For me, it was a really good feeling. Of course, newcomers will get seasick; some only experience it for a short time, others for a long time and some don't suffer at all; it just depends on the person.

I remember, one day, as we were going to the fishing grounds, the two Air Force cadets were so seasick and kept asking to be put ashore. Of course, that would never happen. As time went by, they got used to it and we formed a good friendship.

I was walking about the deck on this beautiful sunny afternoon when I saw one of the Air Force boys asleep on top of the steering chain rack. I felt a bit giddy, as the lad had clearly been on the toilet doing his business when he got a bout of seasickness and managed to scramble onto the deck. What I saw remains with me to this day; the Air Force lad asleep with his trousers not pulled up enough. Then he started vomiting and also, God bless him, having bowel movements without realising! What a mess he was in. I looked around and there was no one nearby, so I woke him up. The look on his face said it all. He ran to the focsle to get cleaned up and when he returned, he was desperate for me not to tell anyone.

I kept the secret forever.

Approximately four days later, we arrived at our destination, south east Iceland, and the nets were put over the side into the sea, (this was called 'shooting the gear'). The weather conditions were good, as there was just a dead swell, no wind. I remember putting on warm clothes, like my father told me to. I had a nice thick, green jersey on, which I was proud of.

When one of the older spare hands saw me with this jersey on, he screamed so much I thought he was going to pass out! "Green! Bloody green, on a ship!" he screamed at me. "You little fool! Get off the deck and put a proper jersey on!" It was some time later that I discovered green clothing to a fisherman is like a red flag to a bull; it just does not work.

I remember suffering from seasickness a little, but not drastically. I was fascinated by the sea and realised that I was actually a 'seadog' in the making.

During the next three weeks, I did what I was told, often covered head to toe in blood and mess from when we caught and gutted the fish, then threw them into the 'washer' to be cleaned with water.

I slept very little, as this new life was so exciting! It seemed unreal, and I knew that sleep would happen later. My friend Tony and I would stay up all hours as we were so involved in what we were doing. I knew this was what I wanted, even though I was just a boy, still wet behind the ears.

When I was on the deck gutting the fish, it was so strange. The crew would tell me to stay inside while we were hauling in the nets and also 'shooting' the nets, as it was so dangerous. As soon as the nets were back in the water, I would take my 'gutting knife' and attempt to dissect the caught fish.

Some of the fish, especially cod, were, to me, like big monsters! Also, if our catch consisted of a lot of catfish, the crew told me to stand in a basket to protect my boots and gloves from their teeth. If a catfish clamped onto your hand, foot, or clothing, it would never let go, so it was so important to keep your feet in the basket!

I spent a lot of time down in the fish room, helping the crew put the fish on layers of ice. It was a difficult job, but I got on with it.

It was the best three weeks ever; perfect for a young boy.

When we arrived back at Hull, my friend and I had to stay out of sight until the ship had berthed at the dock, then we would be in the clear and like any other people visiting their families and friends. So, when the other families of the crew came on board, Tony and I felt relaxed, as we just blended in with the 'visitors'. Then Tony's dad took us in the taxi home to my family. They, of course, quizzed me about what I had done and, being a boy still, I exaggerated my stories a little with my siblings.

The crew had told me to come down to the fish dock the following day and stand outside the office. I did not understand, but nevertheless, I did that, and when the crew members paid off with the result of the catch, they passed me money ('backhanders', like tips) which I appreciated very much. I had never seen so much money before in my life. It was for helping them during the trip but, thinking back, it was *them* who helped *us!* It was certainly an enjoyable time.

So that was the end of my 'pleasure'/work-related trip on the 'Lord Essendon' and I knew I wouldn't forget it for a very long time!

The coming Christmas was when I would be leaving Boulevard High Secondary Modern and going out into the world, where there were 'better things to come'.

During my schooldays, I was friends with lads who were already working on the trawlers, so I would go around with them and they would tell me of all their sea 'experiences'.

Kenny, in particular, would talk about his job, which gave me some insight into what to expect. They were exciting times, but then I got the very bad news that Kenny, as galley boy on a trawler called the 'St Wistan', had been lost at a place called the White Sea, while throwing waste food overboard.

I was devastated as he was a really good friend of mine. I thought of his mam, dad and brother and wondered how they would manage. I was a young boy and thought it was terrible, and yet I was still intent on going to sea.

I visited Kenny's mum and dad to see how they were, and I just cannot say what I felt when I went round to their house; it was terrible. I remember walking away feeling very down about my decisions and the effect they would have on my future.

This was on 8th July 1962. Kenny was 15 years old. God bless him.

Christmas of 1962 arrived and there I was, saying fond farewells to my teachers, classmates and the friends I had accumulated throughout my schooldays.

I spent the Christmas period with my family and, at the end, decided to take a walk down to the fish dock and see the situation of starting work on one of Hull's deep-sea fishing trawlers. I had discussed the prospect with my mother and father (they had been hesitant at first, but then agreed) and now here was the start of my working life.

Some of my school friends came down to the dock with me, and we chatted and compared notes about the best company and ships to work on etc.

The offices were located next door to each other; it was just like walking down a road with shops, but instead of window shopping, I was work shopping! I walked up and down the dock, going into offices and talking to the men who might 'sign' me on. At first, I did not feel too comfortable, as they were telling me I was small and looked young for my age, so I was beginning to feel a little bit down about my situation.

I eventually went into one office called 'Ross Group'. It used to be called 'Stella' which, at that time, was linked with a company based out of Grimsby, across the River Humber. Anyhow, I entered, and the runner's name was Jim Atkinson. He seemed a nice, quiet man, so we got talking and the good thing was that he knew my father.

After about two hours, he agreed to sign me on a trawler called 'Stella Polaris', as galley boy or assistant cook. The title meant nothing to me as I knew I was on the first rung of the ladder and the only way was up.

I left the office and ran home as fast as possible to tell my family the good news. At 15 years and three months, here I was, venturing onto the 'Stella Polaris' as a galley boy looking for fame and fortune!

The 'Stella Polaris', on which I started my first trip as galley boy, aged 15 years and three months. (Skipper Harry Sloane).

I left home during the 2nd week of January 1963 and boarded the 'Stella Polaris'. We sailed for the White Sea, past the coast of Norway. Our 'steaming time' (time to get to the fishing grounds) was about five days.

The cook was a good man who helped me a lot, but then I had to get on with the job, as I was getting paid for it. It was not like the 'pleasure trip', where I was just helping the crew. The first few days, I really thought that I would never return to sea, as the working hours were approximately 5am until about 9pm and the work, especially for a 15-year-old, was gruelling to say the least!

My job was to clean out the cabins, alleyways, officers' rooms and mess room (where we had our meals) with a mop and bucket and assist the cook, which included peeling buckets and buckets of potatoes because, as a crew of over 21, they ate a lot of potatoes!

Believe it or not, something frequently on the menu was, you guessed it, fish! At that time, the price of fish was reasonable, so the owners would 'store up' enough supplies for, say, 25 days, including bacon and eggs, knowing that we could have fish for breakfast when the costly bacon and eggs ran out.

So, on with my job. . .! I remember the shoes I took away. They were heavy and of good quality, but after about two weeks, they were slowly disappearing from my feet. This was due to all the running about I was doing, plus the salt water, so eventually I threw them and had to wear my 'going home' shoes for a while.

I would take sandwiches and tea on the deck to the crew, providing the weather conditions were good. When the weather got bad, it was terrible! The ship rolled from side to side, ducking and diving with the bow. I also had to go onto the bridge to take the skipper or mate cups of tea and when the weather got bad, it felt like something you cannot explain; even worse than the local carnival, on those fast and furious rides where you leave your stomach contents behind!

It must have taken me a good week to settle into some kind of system. The first few days, when I was seasick, the crew would tell me to eat something, as it was straining my stomach. They advised me to eat dry bread, but a lot of the time I was thirsty and felt weak through vomiting, so, silly me, decided I would have a drink of lemonade. As it was trickling down my throat, it felt excellent, then when it touched my stomach, everything backfired, and it all came gushing out again. To put it mildly, I felt bad!

I suppose, like anything, you live and learn, and I really did learn a good lesson from that experience. . .!

As time passed, I got to know the crew and, again, they were all good men. The first few days from the dock, the crew would drink beer and have talks about their families and lives. That was the tradition. Some crew members would get too many drinks inside them and start speaking gibberish, then wander off to their beds, while others would just sit and keep chatting. I remember that, for some unknown reason, fishermen were very good friends and when they got to the fishing part of the trip, they all worked together and looked out for each other. It was amazing to see how they worked as a united team. Fishermen, to me, were a breed of their own, but they united, regardless of any differences.

One of the 'deckie learners' (a deck assistant) was really good to me and we became friends. He would help me with my duties and explain the job to me. His name was David Hunter and we stayed friends for many years to come. (He also told me he was an ex-jockey). As time passed, it was amazing; the people I got the pleasure to work with, from all different backgrounds. I will tell you more, further down the line. The strange thing was that you always knew someone or a 'friend of a friend'. It was a close-knit community.

During my introduction to the deep-sea fishing industry, the trawler owners had employed a training specialist. He was ex-Royal Navy and also ex-commander. (The story will unfold and the ex-commander will appear on my path to success and riches!)

Well, back to reality on board the 'Stella Polaris'; I can say, with all honesty, that those three weeks at sea were the most difficult of my life/career.

Every day was similar to the one before, as there I was, cooped up in the same system. It was hectic; the smells of the engines wafting all around, mixed with the smells of cooking food and fish. It was not a nice combination. My objective, at that moment, was to get up the ladder as fast as possible and escape this working injustice on a 15-year-old boy!

In the evenings, after I finished my work, I would get permission from the cook and the skipper to go on deck and train and help the crew. If the weather was good, I would help the crew gut the fish or, sometimes, I would go down to the fish room. As time went on, I was training to become a deckie learner.

I did the three-week trip on the 'Stella Polaris' and returned to the port. I went down to the dock office to collect my earnings; my weekly pay at that time was five pounds, which I thought was the beginning of a fortune! I was also told to stand outside the office and wait for the crew members to come down to settle up on their earnings.

When each member received his settlings, he would approach me and give me between one and five pounds; 'backhanders'. I also found out that I would depend on my weekly wage and the backhanders until I was 'good enough' to go onto poundage (which meant I would get a small percentage of the catch).

The backhanders were a trawling tradition to help galley boys boost their wages and, of course, the better the galley boy worked, the greater the tips he would get. So I was very pleased, and when I counted up my backhanders, I knew I would be returning to the 'Stella Polaris' for a further trip to sea and that my future would be in the fishing industry.

I did return to the 'Stella Polaris' as galley boy once more and, again, was put through my paces. It was a minimum working day of 15 hours and, at 15 years old, it was a case of keeping your head down and getting on with the job.

**The 'Man O War' was one of the ships I worked on
as galley boy. (Skipper Billy Jopling).**

The galley boy capacity lasted for a total of six trips. I did a further two in a trawler called 'Man O War' and, believe me, I really thought she was a 'Man O War', she was that old! I did other trips on ships called the 'Lord Alexander' and the 'Lord Tedder'. On both of these trawlers, the skipper was a man from Iceland called Enevoldson, or something similar, but for some unknown reason, he was called Teager or Eager Teager.

**The 'Lord Alexander', another one of the ships I worked on
as a galley boy. (Skipper Harold Enevoldsen). Later,
I sailed as mate with skipper Maurice Ward.**

19

Having completed the six trips as galley boy, I thought the time was right to start looking for promotion and trying to get on deck as a deckie learner.

I signed on a vessel called 'Benvolio' in October 1963, which was owned by a company called Hellyer Brothers, later to become a part of BUT (British United Trawlers). I would go on to spend quite a bit of my trawling career with this company.

Chapter 2

DECKIE LEARNER START

I went to sea on board the 'Benvolio' and the skipper was called Ben Ashcroft. The crew members were very good; they helped me, as everyone on board knew that it was my first trip on deck and yes, they played some jokes, but it was a learning curve, so I tried to take it in my stride. I completed three trips on board the 'Benvolio'. I remember we carried two deckie learners, which created a sense of competition.

The good thing for me was that my father was also a fisherman who had a very good name, so he was well-respected by many and, of course, when the crew members realised who my father was, it made my life somewhat easier. Let's not forget that Hull was a relatively small city, with a population of some 300,000, and the fishing industry was, at that time, a big industry, which included people working on the fish market, lorry drivers, buyers, sellers and numerous others. So, it employed a lot of Hull people; also, a great number of those who lived on Hessle Road and nearby.

The 'Benvolio'; my first trip as deckie learner.
(Skipper Ben Ashcroft).

Well, back to the 'Benvolio' and yes, the voyage went well but yes, it was hard, as we caught a lot of fish. With all the work, I think I came off the ship with my back feeling the same shape as a banana!

A gentleman called Commander Beale was the training officer. All the galley boys and deckie learners had to visit him, as on each trip, the skipper would forward an assessment report to this gentleman, to see if the galley boys and deckie learners would be capable of continuing in the deep-sea fishing industry.

It was around this time that I got the devastating news that my friend, Tony Martin, who had taken a 'pleasure trip' with me on the 'Lord Essendon' and been deckie learner on the 'Kingston Pearl', had had a terrible accident and died from his injuries. I was so upset. I just could not believe it; he was just 16 years old. His fatal accident happened on 30th November 1964. It gave me food for thought. . . should I carry on, or get a safer job somewhere else. . .?

So now I will return to the eventful meeting with our so-called 'training officer'.

As soon as I saw the gentleman, I felt uneasy and apprehensive, as I knew that he knew nothing of the job, a trawler's design or how they performed, as he was ex-Royal Navy, not ex-trawlerman. We had a conversation and at the end, he abruptly said to me, "Have you ever thought about being a bricklayer?"

This really took the wind out of my sails. I felt terrible, embarrassed and humiliated. On the other hand, I was fired up to show this so-called naval officer what the trawling industry was all about.

This Commander Beale's summary was something I would never forget; I only wish that the same gentleman had been around a few years later. I was approaching my 16th birthday, by which time I knew I would be a fully-fledged fisherman.

When we got home, after each trip, I would gather my friends; quite a few of whom had their sights set on a future on board the Hull trawlers. Like any other 16-year-old lad, I thought I was the best and could do everything better than anyone else and yes, I did sneak into pubs with my friends and have a 'couple of pints'. Back then, I thought I was invincible! The next morning, I'd realise I was not.

Chapter 3

JEANNIE HAWKER AND HER FAMILY

I started courting a very nice girl, who was also from Hessle Road. Her name was Jean Hawker, but she was known as Jeannie. I had known Jeannie for four months and to me she was very special. I knew that I would marry Jeannie as it just seemed right, even at our young ages. I really thought we were just meant for each other.

Yes, I really did love Jeannie, and we started to court seriously, and then Jeannie told me about her father, God bless him. Jean's father was also a fisherman. He was a bosun. Unfortunately, a few months before, he had been lost at sea, so I never got to meet Jean's dad, which became a big void in my life.

Jeannie told me that her dad had been lost overboard on the Hull trawler, 'St Giles', and again, it was a bad feeling I got, especially for Jean, as her mum was left with seven children. It was so upsetting. Jean's dad was lost at Spitzbergen Grounds on the 8th August 1963. The report said an O'Kettle had pulled Jean's dad overboard. O'Kettle was just a name which us fisherman used, but I believe it was some kind of a basking shark which just laid on the seabed and ate plankton, but they grew to large sizes and it was not good to catch one in the trawl. The shark was not a fierce fish, it was just big, and very heavy, and the equivalent to having massive stones in the net. The net just gets pulled back in the water and unfortunately, that is what happened to Jean's dad. It was so sad for Jean and her family. I could really picture how it may have happened, and for it to happen to a man who was just 40 years old, leaving behind his really nice wife, children and friends; it was ever so sad. Then, deep down, I knew I would grow closer and closer to Jean as time went on, as she was a nice girl and I really thought a lot of her. I really felt sad for Jean's mam, as it was so difficult for a widow to raise children; especially seven! I would listen to Kitty (Jean's mam) tell me nice stories of herself and Jean's dad when they were courting, and also when they first got married. It was like, this is what Jean and I are going to do! Yes, we were following in Jean's mam and dad's footsteps. So strange!

For me, it was just a matter of time. For sure, I would ask Jean to be my wife (at that moment, I was hoping Jean would agree to my thoughts!) Jean and I stayed together as, for me, she was the best, and we would do what all couples did at that time. Time was of the essence, as I would be at sea for about 21 days, then home for three days, and back to sea, so yes, I treasured my time with Jean as I loved her very much.

Jean was and still is a very good dancer, but I must admit, I was a bit clumsy to say the least! However, I would take Jean to the dance halls around Hull and we would spend some really nice times together. Sometimes Jean would have her friends and I would have mine, so we would all meet up together at a dance place and then just wander off with each other. For me, looking back at those times, life was simple but good. I remember a café on Hessle Road called Blue Spot. This was where we would meet up with each other, then decide where to go, either in pairs or all together.

Jean had five siblings, including identical twin brothers, and they were a handful when they were younger! They grew up and did very well in their careers. Jean's sisters married seamen also and so, really, Jean's family were married to seafarers and her dad, God bless him, left a good legacy.

I would go away to sea and send Jean telegrams (the mode of communication at that time) and I could not wait to be with her. Yes, it was a nice feeling, as there I was at sea, doing a man's job (or nearly!) and going home to see my nice girlfriend.

Well, the time passed by and yes, I was steadily learning the job and progressing slowly, but surely, at this time, I was feeling good and my next step up would be in a spare hand capacity, which was deckhand, and my wages and poundage would double!

Jean (now my beautiful wife) and I at Hull Fair, October 1965.

Jean and I at Hull Fair, October 2018.

I considered myself good at my job, but knew there was always room for improvement, so I signed on as deckie learner on 'St Crispin', which was owned by Boston Deep-Sea Fishing, formerly St Andrews Steam Fishing. I did three trips on board the 'St Crispin', and the job got better and easier as time went by. The crew on board were very good; young men, but nice to work with and learn from.

'St Crispin'. (Skipper Ray Richardson).

'Loch Moidart'. (Skipper Gil Casson).

Above is the good old 'Loch Moidart' just going through the lock pits at St Andrew's Dock. I was deckie learner.

After the 'St Crispin', I decided to go back to Hellyer Brothers (which later became BUT (British United Trawlers). I signed on a vessel called 'Loch Moidart' and the skipper's name was Gil Casson. He treated me very well and allowed me a 'dram' of rum per day, which all the crew had for 'medicinal purposes'. The other deckie learner, who was the same age as me, was not allowed this rum ration as per the skipper's orders. He said the deckie learner did not do enough work to deserve it!

I stayed with this ship for two trips, then started to get itchy feet, so signed off and went to see if I could sign on a better and newer trawler. I then signed on a ship called 'James Barrie' of Newington's Fishing Company. It looked about the same age as 'Loch Moidart' and the skipper was called Dick Taylor, who, later on, became notorious.

'James Barrie'. (Skipper Dickie Taylor).

I must say, the two trips I did were good, as on one of the trips, we had pleasurers on board, which reminded me of my 'pleasure trip!' It was good to have them, as I was still a young boy myself.

I remember when the snow blizzards came. A lot of seabirds were blinded and crashed into the masts. My job was to get hold of them and throw them back into the air. So off I popped, and Robert Glenton was one of the pleasurers who came with me.

I was brought up with the Glentons, down Eastbourne Street, off Hessle Road, and Robert's dad, Billy, had a wet fish shop on Hessle Road for years. Eventually Billy Junior took over from his dad and sadly it was closed down last year (2017) when Billy Junior passed away. I know he will be sadly missed.

So, when young Robert came on board it was good fun, and it just brought back all those memories with the seagulls (we called them Mollys; I still do not know why we called them that!) The first one I caught just turned its head 180 degrees and bit my hand! I let it go in shock. It managed to take flight and get away, but there were lots of them, just dropping onto our decks. We certainly learned from our first bird. It was funny.

The second trip was just unbelievable, as I had a bad tooth, and of course an abscess formed which, at sea, is the last thing you need! As the skipper's knowledge was not the best (no disrespect), I just had to do my job as best I could. Needless to say, as soon as I got home, the tooth was extracted!

'St Chad'. (Skipper Ray Richardson).

I did two trips on board 'St Chad' as deckie learner, and when I think back to all the crew I sailed with, they were really good and it was certainly an industry where you all looked after one another. The skipper Ray Richardson eventually became mate with me when we were in the oil and gas industry many years later.

'St Matthew'. (Skipper Peter Craven).

Then, after two trips, I went back to St Andrews and signed on the 'St Matthew', which was a big, conventional trawler. She was a very fast ship! I believe, at full speed, with very heavy consumption, she could do 17 knots. For a trawler, this was really fast. I remember we were coming home from the White Sea fishing grounds and didn't have a good-sized catch on board, so the atmosphere was not too good.

We had 24-36 hours spare, so the skipper decided to have a 'feel around' at a bank in the North Sea, at the south end of Norway, called Halten Bank. It was known as a place where you could kill a few hours, and the ground was a smooth seabed, so you knew you wouldn't damage your nets. In general, it was OK, providing the weather conditions were good.

Well, believe it or not, we shot the trawl and, like I said, the 'St Matthew' was a big trawler and after a few tows, both sides of the foredeck were full to the gunwales! I had never seen so many fish in my life, and they were all coley (part of the cod family).

When our spare fishing time was up, we secured the trawl and commenced gutting and cleaning the fish. All hands were working on this operation!

At 17 years old, I was on the deck continuously for about 36 hours (apart from 10-minute tea breaks every four or five hours) and covered from head to foot in coley guts and blood. I felt that my back was the same shape as a net hook! The mate told me to go and get a shower, then turn in for a few hours. I am a big believer in 'always obey the last command'!

I took my shower then 'crawled' into my bed, and that was all I remember! 36 hours later I awoke and thought it had all been a dream, then reality came back to me, along with the aches.

When I went back on deck, the crew joked and said they thought I had died! All the fish had been cleaned and put down in the fish room, so all we had to do was clean the decks and get everything secure for steaming home to Hull.

When we were coming down the River Humber, there was a Grimsby trawler which was slowly but surely passing us, and all the Grimsby lads were on deck shouting and booing at us! I thought, "I wish our skipper would give the engines full speed, just for a few moments, and we could zoom by this bunch of Grimmys!" I think our skipper was having the same thought as we suddenly felt our ship vibrating, and it was just like a greyhound passing a tortoise; we passed the Grimsby ship with ease! It was a very good feeling for us on board; we could see all the Grimsby lads walking off the deck, feeling humiliated. Yes, it was good.

The weekly wage for a deckie learner was about eight pounds a week, plus a small percentage of the ship's catch, and for spare hands, the weekly wage was 11 pounds per week, and for every 1000 pounds the catch brought, a spare hand would get 13 shillings. The more money the catch brought, the bigger the pay-off for all the crew.

We landed our trip from the 'St Matthew' and I did well financially, but yet again, I was still interested in other companies.

I signed on the 'St Keverne' for two trips and the skipper was called John Gibson. These were good trips, but again, I was itching for better prospects.

'St Keverne'. (Skipper John Gibson).

'Ross Adair'. (Skipper Ted Bilton).

I was deckie learner on the 'Cape Adair' (later renamed 'Ross Adair') for two hard trips, which were well-paid. I was realising there were no easy trips at all!

'St Alcuin'. (Skipper Fred Barwick/Kenny Rose).

I signed on the 'St Alcuin', which belonged to Thomas Hamling Company, as deckie learner and did a total of four trips on board this vessel.

I was learning all the time; especially from the people I met, from different towns and cities around the UK.

On my first trip on board the 'St Alcuin', the crew was good and, in all honesty, the crews from fishing trawlers were like a race of people different to anyone else. Sometimes you did not really know the people, but within three or four days, you would be putting your life on the line for them if need be, and they would be doing the same for you. I suppose there was a special bond within the trawlermen.

Some of the crew members were really good people. I remember one lad who came from Fleetwood; he was a great bloke. He used to teach me all sorts of things, especially net-mending. Apparently, the people of Fleetwood were the best at net-mending!

Anyway, back to Tom Bissett, the Fleetwood man, who was a spare hand. He was living in Hull, single and a 'man about town'. He was courting this local girl who, to put it mildly, was a very friendly girl. Well, Tom had been courting this girl for quite a while and I think the novelty was wearing off for him. On this particular trip, he told me that when we got tied up in the fish dock, he would take his 'heavy gear' off with him and go back to Fleetwood for a few months. So I said, "Tom, what about your girlfriend?"

Tom said that when we approached the dockside, if I saw his girlfriend, I had to tell her that Tom had been put ashore earlier on for medical reasons.

So Tom got out of sight when we were approaching the jetty and I could see his girlfriend. She had a bottle of whisky in her hand. Then all of a sudden, she shouted at top note, "Tommy, darling, I have got you a bottle!"

No more to be said; I saw Tom running onto the whaleback (front of the ship), shouting, "OK my darling! I will be with you soon!"

I turned around to Tom and said, "What about your plan?" He said the thought of the bottle of whisky had changed his mind!

Anyhow, we got into St Andrew's Dock and Tom went off with his girlfriend, as we all went our different ways. I went home to my mam and dad, until we met up onshore the following day, when we settled up on the dock.

After a few days, we were ready to sail once more on the 'St Alcuin'. Fortunately, the mate who was on board was the skipper of the 'Lord Essendon' when I stowed away at 14 years old; Kenny Rose.

The trawler was built in the 1950s, so it was not too bad. My last trip was certainly one to remember! The skipper's name was Fred Barwick and he was a good person. The skipper on this trip (which was to be his last on the 'St Alcuin' – meaning he would be signed off and go on board another trawler) took us to Greenland. The ship was old and not a very good sea ship.

I remember, when we went to the east coast of Greenland, the skipper would take the ship very close to the shore, towing the trawl, and then turn around and come back out, away from the shoreline, and haul the nets. There was nothing to shout about, regarding the quantity of the catch, but anything was better than nothing.

Anyhow, I will continue the story!

As the time passed at east Greenland, the ice flow was starting to come down and the skipper would tow close to the ice, as the fish were below it. Some hauls were good and some less so, but the skipper persevered. . . until the time came when it was too late! We got trapped in the ice and there was nothing we could do about it, especially as we were fishing alone, with no other trawlers in the vicinity!

We managed to haul our nets and get them secure, but there was no way we could escape, as we were not powerful enough to crash through the ice.

So there we were, in the North Atlantic Arctic Circle, surrounded by miles and miles of ice, trapped, and with no other vessel in sight. We were certainly up the creek!

We were getting tighter and tighter; the trawlers built in that era were of rivet design, so the more we got pressed into the ice, the more the rivets started to break out. They began to leak slightly; we were bailing the stern steering compartment and time was passing quickly.

We got some news that our company's newest vessel (a brand-new stern trawler), 'St Finbarr', was on its way to 'break us out'. We felt very good, as we had been trapped for about 14 days and were beginning to get very nervous.

Eventually, the 'St Finbarr' did come to rescue us. To see her coming was reassuring; what a ship she looked! Very big, and of course she was brand new.

The 'St Finbarr' came close to us and passed us, towing lines and wires, and we got connected up and, of course, all this took time, as we were fishing vessels, not towing tugs! Nevertheless, we got on with it.

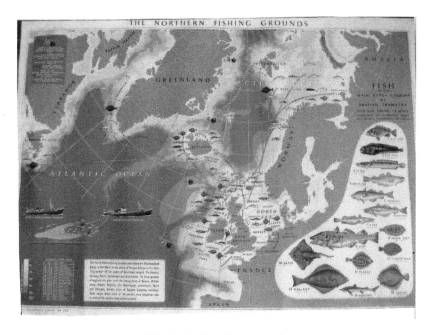

North Atlantic grounds

Eventually we were connected and underway. The agreement was to tow us back to Reykjavik, Iceland, where we could be repaired correctly and efficiently.

After five days of being towed by the 'St Finbarr', we arrived at Reykjavik and the fish we had caught at Greenland was discharged and sold there. This happened for two reasons; first, because the quality of the fish would decline, and second, we had to take the weight from the ship so that we could get up to the slipway.

As soon as the discharging of the fish was finished, the 'St Alcuin' was pulled out of the water onto the slipway.

A note on the 'St Finbarr'. . . she went on to do some really good trips, but unfortunately, on Christmas Day 1966, she was fishing off Newfoundland and there was a terrible fire on board, claiming the lives of 11 crew members.

This was the first time I had seen a trawler on the slipway and, to me, she looked massive! Anyhow, things started happening i.e. dockworkers came to repair the damage and of course all the crew stayed on the ship and tried to keep the ship reasonably clean. In those times, a normal trawler trip would take about 18-21 days, depending on the fishing grounds, but we all knew it was going to take us a lot longer than that.

We finally got all the repairs completed, loaded bunkers and provisions etc. then just prior to sailing, the skipper started talking about us returning to where we had come from! This, of course, was Greenland. We all knew this would not be right and that we would be away from our families for a long time.

Telephone calls were made between the skipper, the owners and the mate (remember he had also sailed as skipper previously?)

After much haggling, the skipper was signed off the ship's articles and left the ship. The mate took control.

So we sailed again, departing Reykjavik. As the mate was familiar with the fishing grounds, we stopped not too far off and 'shot the nets' at a place called Snowy (named after the high mountains, covered in snow, which could be picked on the ship's radar).

So away went the nets. The weather was not too bad, so we settled back into our normal fishing routine.

We stayed in the general area for about a week and had a total of about 1200 kits (each kit weighing 10 stone) which, under the circumstances, was not too bad. The owners then informed us to return to Hull, which we did without complaint and, like I said earlier, the normal voyage length was between 18 and 21 days, and ours took 42! It was the longest trip any of the crew had done before.

The next day, when I went down to the office at the dock to 'settle up', I think I came away with about 10 pounds, which to me was scandalous! I did also get my weekly wage, but to settle with 10 pounds, after all we went through, was just unfair. I was not alone in my opinion, so I signed off the mighty 'St Alcuin' and started looking for better prospects.

Later on, I will explain more about settling wages and percentages, as it can go the other way, too.

Chapter 4

JEAN AND I GET MARRIED

So we will continue with my story, as I venture along to promotion.

In the year 1966, in the month of April, Jean and I were to be married! We knew but we loved each other so much. We got married on the 2nd April 1966.

Life was good, but, in the position of deckie learner, things could have been better. I wanted to do my best for my beautiful wife and, hopefully, our future children.

I was afraid Jeannie might refuse to marry me, because her dad was lost at sea a few months before we met (I will tell you more about Jean's dad further on in the book) and I was worried she might be afraid of losing another loved one. But we went ahead and got married in Fisherman's Bethel on Hessle Road, which once stood near Boulevard. The chaplain Mr Chappel married us.

Despite being young, we knew marriage was the right decision and had a lot of support from Jean's mum. I thought it was really good of Jean's mum to be behind us, as she was still hurting from losing Stan, her husband.

Life was simple but there were also lots of sad moments.

When we first married, we lived in a flat above a small business off Clifton Street, Beverley Road. I'll always remember the day I was sailing on the 'Dunsley Wyke' and Jean was waiting to get some hospital checks. We stayed in the flat for a short while, then Jean got us a small terraced house known as a two-up two-down, which was down Wainfleet Terrace, off Fountain Road, Beverley Road. In fact, it was just behind the hospital, and between the hospital and our terrace was Barmston Drain and yes, people used to canoe up and down! Oh, how life has changed!

I was always thinking about Jean when I was away at sea, wondering how she was coping. In those days, the telegram was the only method of communication. I knew her mam was helping her a lot, though. I know Jean used to worry a lot, especially with her dad getting lost overboard; that must have been devastating. Jean's mam tried to get some kind of financial help from the trawler owners, as she had six children to bring up on her own. The sad and disgraceful thing outcome was that the courts said the incident was 'an act of God', therefore there was no compensation or pay-out. I am so disgusted with the British system; thousands of families from Hull suffered the same sadness and yet the Hull trawler owners got away without any legal obligations to the distressed families. So sad.

Now I was becoming a man! I knew I would push myself to seek promotion, so that I could take good care of my new wife. Up to this point, I had only sailed as deckie learner, so had to take a 'big step' and show the fishing industry that I was starting to ascend the ladder of success!

My wife was behind me 100 per cent and, as her father had been a fisherman, Jean knew that I would be at sea for a lot of our lives, but also that this would bring us a better lifestyle.

Jean and I on our Wedding Day, 2nd April 1966, at Fishermen's Bethel, Hessle Road.

So, at the ripe old age of 18, I got my 'start' as spare hand with Hellyer Brothers. The trawler's name was 'Dunsley Wyke' and she too, god bless, was an old lady of the sea.

Once on board, I realised that I knew quite a lot of the crew, as we had sailed together before. With this class of ship (old), you tend to get a crew of younger men (green?) but we stuck together and did a good job. We all kept each other safe.

It was challenging, but also an ego boost for me. I remember that the bosun, Ken Gibson, when the work was consistent on deck, would say, "Go aft and get a cup of tea" and so off we went for a well-deserved break.

We would all line up for a cup of tea, get the tea in our hands and sit down and, bearing in mind it was boiling hot, he would come in, get his, down it in one gulp and say, "Come on then, let's be having you!" and we were back on the deck again for another long period.

'Dunsley Wyke'. (Skippers: Kenny Thresh,
Eric Green, Ronnie Crickmore).

I remember that the ship, which had accommodation aft (sleeping cabins etc.) was classed as 'paradise'. Ships which had accommodation forward were not exactly what you needed! When the weather was not good, when you were going to take your steaming watch (on the bridge), you would get woken up 15 minutes before your watch time and have to get out of a nice warm bed, get dressed into your oilskins then run along the foredeck and into the after part of the vessel where you got 'unrigged', before going onto the bridge and relieving the watch who were going below.

Please remember, the weather conditions were really bad and so all the watch going on would group together, as it was the safest way to get from the focsle to the bridge, and the same for the watch going below. You were never alone, especially in bad weather, as a rule of thumb.

It certainly was not nice when the wind could go above force 10. The people on the bridge (officers of the watch) would watch carefully and reduce the vessel's speed, then we would make a run for it to the after accommodation. When we left St Andrew's Dock, we would always 'rig up' lifelines to get hold of in the event of waves crashing on board. So, as you can appreciate, if you were on a ship with after sleeping, you could just walk through the engine room and onto the bridge, dressed only in slippers and casual gear. So it really was much more comfortable to be working on a 'paradise' ship! I only had such luck as a galley boy or deckie learner.

This was the beginning of an episode which 'sorted the men from the boys'!

I bade goodbye to my new wife, who was having our first child, so I was a little bit apprehensive! Looking back, she was not much more than a child herself. It was the month of June 1966 when our first baby was born. We named her Deborah. What a beautiful little baby.

The system seemed to be that, in the older ships, the crews were much younger than the 'well-experienced' crews, who would get the opportunity to work on the newer, bigger and better trawlers. Of course, the newer trawlers were faster, so they could reach the fishing grounds a lot quicker and the crew had more time on the grounds, enabling them to earn more money than those on the older, slower trawlers.

Enough said of that! Here I was, on board, and it was the biggest step of my career, so it was up to me to do the job to the best of my ability.

With the 'Dunsley Wyke' being a smaller trawler, we sailed to Iceland and commenced fishing on the south east side. It took us three to four days to get to our destination; weather being good, of course. In my mind, I knew that, whatever the outcome, I had to accept the dangerous work and continue, as I had my wife and daughter to think about. I was still a young bloke, but I knew I had to give it my best, as it was not that easy, getting work on the trawlers. My dad and Jean's dad had had good names in the industry, and I certainly did not want to let them down. I knew I would make it, as I felt it was meant to be; me going to sea and providing for my lovely wife and child.

The trip went well, and I felt accomplished. I did about six trips on the 'Dunsley Wyke' (an average of three weeks per trip). We did not make much money, but at least I was getting a good experience and my wife was receiving a weekly wage, so I could start looking for a bigger and better ship.

I will never forget my last trip on board the 'Dunsley Wyke'. I had been promoted to fish room man and one of my jobs was heaving the bags of fish in, using the wires on the port side of the winch. My station was on the lee side on the port side of the ship, as we had to haul and shoot the trawl on the weather side so that the wind would push the ship away from the trawl and we would not catch it in the propeller. This particular time, the winchman was a Polish chap. All the crew used to call him 'Lurch'; he had size 16 feet, hence his name.

He was at the winch controls when my wires got crossed (called a 'riding turn') and my hand became trapped. I shouted to the winchman to stop the winch. By this time, I had been taken three times at least around the winch barrel and it felt as if something in my chest had broken. It was agonising.

As the winchman was inexperienced, he reversed the winch and it took me back the other way. It was at that time I blacked out.

When I came around, crew members were carrying me to the mess room. The skipper, Eric Green (who had the nickname Erky) came down and told me he was taking me to Iceland to see the doctor. My ribcage was killing me and I could not straighten my back, so the crew gave me a couple of pillows, so I could rest my head. I was in and out of sleep, sitting up.

The skipper took me to a port called Seydisfjord, then to the local hospital, where the doctor confirmed that I could not return to the ship, so it sailed without me.

For the first few days, it was terrible. The food consisted of fish with jam and some other unmentionable products, but I managed to get by.

I was to be repatriated. The doctor said that I had very badly bruised my ribs, but thankfully nothing was broken.

I remember, when I flew back to London, Heathrow, I was carrying my holdall with three weeks' worth of work clothes inside, and with my bruised ribs, it was agonising. I managed to drag myself and my bag to Kings Cross train station and get on the train.

It was so nice to see my wife waiting for me when we pulled into Hull train station. I laid my case on our baby's pram and we took a nice slow walk home, with me explaining to my wife what had happened. Of course, she was really upset, but I assured her that nothing would ever happen to me again.

Word got around that if I had attempted to take my case to court, I would never have got another job with BUT. Thinking back, I should have gone to court to see what would have happened.

I stayed at home for about four weeks, until I felt good enough to go back to sea and the sea doctor (Doctor Burns) had cleared me to go.

**'Kingston Sardius' in Kingston Colours.
(Skippers: Brian Lee and Billy Ward).**

I then signed on the vessel 'Kingston Sardius', which I was very pleased about, as this was me starting to climb up the ladder! I completed five trips on the 'Kingston Sardius', then got a better break in 1967 and signed on a vessel called the 'Kingston Peridot' as spare hand. It was a bit better than the 'Kingston Sardius', even though they were sister ships; still an old class vessel and, again the accommodation was forward, but I was determined to get going with my future and start aiming for 'bigger things'.

1968 saw the tragic triple sinking of the three Hull trawlers 'Ross Cleveland', 'St Romanus' and 'Kingston Peridot'.

**'Kingston Peridot'. (Skippers: Billy Ward,
Albert Reagan, Ray Wilson).**

I did four trips on the 'Kingston Peridot'; one of which is very memorable. We were dodging the seas as there was very bad weather. The watch had been relieved and we all ran forward (under the watchful eye of the bosun). One of the spare hands came following us in the focsle and what happened was amazing.

This spare hand, Mike, (from Whitby), stood there in the doorway with a sandwich in his hand, then suddenly the ship dipped her bow into the trough of the sea. As she was coming out of the trough, it seemed like an invisible force got hold of Mike, picked him up and held him in mid-air! Then, all of a sudden, the ship lurched to the port side and seemed to throw Mike that way. It seemed very unnatural.

Mike dropped to the floor and the ship's movements seemed to ease, so we ran across to Mike. He had a cut above his eye, but apart from that, he was a very lucky man! I think Mike's sandwich ended up in my lap.

So, after four trips on the 'Kingston Peridot', I decided to look for a better ship. As you can see, I was staying with BUT rather than move from company to company. I wanted them to know I was a stable and reliable person who they could depend on. I was very proud to say that I had never been 'sacked', so yes, I was feeling good.

'Ross Anson'. (Skipper Harry Sanderson).

I decided to take a chance and went with Ross's. At this time, they had not amalgamated with Hellyer Brothers and Jimmy Atkinson. The company's runner was a nice chap; he had given me my start as a galley boy on the 'Stella Polaris', so he signed me on as spare hand of the 'Ross Anson'. This trawler had been in Grimsby, so they decided to send it to Hull. The skipper's name was Harry Sanderson and he seemed alright to me, even though we had heard some not so good stories about him. I knew quite a few of the crew, who were around my age, so it was not too bad.

I remember one time we had a Ouija board. I could not accept what it said, so I walked out and the other lads were shouting, "Come back, Ken, it's telling the truth!" Looking back, it was good fun.

I think the cook on board was of Asian descent and a strange person to say the least! We were steaming to the White Sea and the food up till then had been absolutely terrible. So early one morning, when my two watch mates and I came off watch, we broke into the pantry. I know this is unlawful, but try telling that to three young seamen who are absolutely starving!

Anyhow, we broke in and got eggs, bacon, bread and coffee (which, in those days, came in large tins). Well, we had our fry-up and it was great! We really enjoyed our 'illegal breakfast'! So we

48

cleaned the dishes, put everything back in its correct place and went to our bunks, contented. This was at 4am and at midday, we were back on watch, so we went into the galley/mess room to get a quick lunch before going on deck. There was a serving hatch into the galley and when we put our faces close to the hatch, the cook would appear from the other side and say, "Soup! You want f***ing soup!" so really he was not a nice chap.

Well, we sat down in the galley and out of the corner of my eye, I saw the coffee tin and knew then that our fate was sealed! We must have left it out when we had our slap-up meal! I made motions to my two watch mates and we decided to pretend we hadn't noticed.

While everyone was eating, the cook then came into the mess room for idle chit-chat and all of a sudden, he must have seen the tin of coffee (bearing in mind that all food stuffs were very limited) because he just snapped! He came hurtling up to the table and smashed his fist through the tin! There were coffee dust everywhere. Me and my two mates did not waste time wondering what was going to happen; the cook looked at us, pulled out the longest knife I had ever seen from the back of his waist belt and started chasing us around the deck! (I know we may have been able to overpower him, but with a knife like a machete, you may be unlucky).

We ran onto the bridge and the skipper screamed "What the f*** is going on?" Immediately, the cook shot in the bridge. We, plus the radio operator and the skipper wrestled the cook to the floor, then some of the other crew came and tied him up.

Now I think it was funny, but at the time I can assure you it was not! Eventually the safest thing to do was for the skipper to call the police when we went into the port in Norway. They took him away, to the hospital or prison. I never did see that man again.

So, again, I decided to return to BUT, as they seemed to be good with me, so off I went and again signed on the 'Kingston Peridot'.

On the first trip, the skipper was called Billy Ward and later on, I became mate with his brother Maurice on the 'Portia'.

See below the 'Kingston Peridot' when she was in her 'Kingston colours'. When Kingston later amalgamated with Hellyer Brothers, then eventually became BUT, they painted their ships grey.

Kingston Peridot in 'Kingston colours'. (Skipper Billy Ward).

At the end of 1967, I signed off the 'Kingston Peridot' and, a few days later, signed on the 'Kingston Garnet'. What was to follow was the strangest thing I had experienced up to then. . . I found out that the 'Kingston Peridot' had mysteriously disappeared and was reported lost. All the crew members were reported missing.

**Kingston Garnet in 'Kingston colours'.
(Skippers: Brian Lee and Ronnie Bunce).**

Chapter 5

LEAD UP TO THE
TRIPLE TRAWLER TRAGEDY

I remember that the lead up to 1968 and the events of that year were strange, as there were some trawlers which never carried a radio operator, for some unknown reason! Also there was a Hull lady, Lily Bilocca, who was involved in the fishing industry as a worker and had a son, Ernie, who was a fisherman. Lily got the fisherman's wives, mothers, girlfriends and families to band together and they went on demonstration campaigns for better working conditions for the fisherman. They pressed and pressed and yes, the women from Hull did a very good job for their loved ones who were fishermen. The good thing for me, in 1968, was that my wife gave birth to our second child; another beautiful daughter, who we named Lisa Marie. Lisa was born on the 16th November.

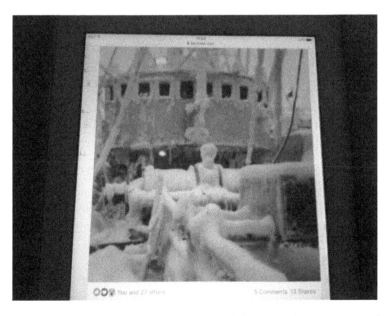

Photograph of typical icy conditions, fishing in the Arctic Circle.

In 1968, Hull's worst fishing trawler disaster occurred when three trawlers went down. Only one man was rescued.

Brian Lee, the skipper on the 'Kingston Garnet', had been in command of the 'Kingston Sardius', so he knew my capabilities and asked me if I would go with him. This was a very big boost for me, so I was eager to sign on with Brian.

I would like it to be known that the 'Kingston Garnet' was unofficially a 'white elephant'. For what reason, I do not know, but that was the story going around the fish dock. Also, it was known for not being a very good sea ship, i.e. it would roll on a damp cloth; that was the crew's reaction.

Well, whatever the thoughts were, here I was on board and away we sailed to Iceland. The skipper was very experienced and thought highly of his crew, so it was up to the crew to have faith in the skipper and do our jobs the best we could.

I did two trips with skipper Brian Lee and we were doing well for money. We were competing with the other vessels fishing in our area, so all was going to plan.

It was the winter of 1968 and we were fishing off the North Cape of Iceland. The weather was absolutely terrible; it was easily force 10, if not more, and black frost covered the UK, with other countries in the same situation. I was spare hand but had come on leaps and bounds with my experience and by the time this trip was finished, I would be brimming with self-confidence.

At this time, we had on board approximately 700 kits of fish (each kit weighed 10 stone) so the prospects were not looking good, but also, to be fair, we could have been in a much worse position.

When the trawlers were at their home port, they filled up with fresh ice for the forthcoming catch, as well as fuel, oil, water and supplies. This was based on the assumption that the trip would average between 21 and 25 days. Consequently, while the trawlers were fishing (towing their equipment on the seabed), of course, they were consuming fuel, and as the fish were caught, it would compensate for the burning of fuel. So, as long as the trawlers were catching fish, the stability of the vessels would remain intact.

Problems would arise if, for example, the weather was too bad, and the trawlers could not catch fish, but fuel was still being consumed. It would put the trawlers in an unsafe and unstable situation. Plus, when the weather conditions were really bad i.e. freezing and ice accumulating aloft, the trawlers would become 'top heavy', so the object was to keep the masts clear at all times, or else there was a very big possibility of the trawler 'turning turtle'; rolling over in a matter of minutes.

Chapter 5A

THE BEGINNING OF THE
TRIPLE TRAWLER TRAGEDY

So now I will return to that day at the North Cape of Iceland on board the Hull trawler 'Kingston Garnet'. The weather was atrocious, and I was on duty, along with another spare hand, and the officer of the watch was the third hand, who was one step below the bosun.

As I briefly explained previously, the objective was to keep the ships stable, so as we burned fuel and consumed stores, we would replace the weights with our catch (fish). So yes, it was a dangerous situation, but the skippers were very experienced, so we put our trust and faith in them, and our lives on the line.; the industry was ranked the most dangerous in the world! Again, I must stress that, on board our ship, the 'Kingston Garnet', the majority of the deck crew were young men still seeking their future in the deep-sea fishing industry. Myself, I have never ever seen weather as bad as it was during that period. We were scrambling for our lives.

One night will remain with me till I die. We were trying to run the vessel under the 'lee', which meant that we were running into safe area and shelter until the bad weather passed. There must have been about another 30 trawlers in the same predicament. I was on the bridge and the skipper and mate, as expected, were there too. We were in a dangerous situation, as we had only 700 kits on board, so our stability was not as good as it should have been; we had been away from our home port for a good while.

Our radar was slowing down due to the adverse weather and the ice was really setting aloft. Me and my watch mate were doing turns on the bridge top to free the radar scanner of ice so that we could get a picture on the radar screen of the surroundings, which the skipper could use to navigate the ship down the Icelandic Fjord to Isafjord and safety. At that moment, we could hear other vessels in our area, on the VHF and further. They were all in trouble, whether from wind or ice.

We heard a call from one Grimsby vessel (called 'Boston' something, I think). The vessel radio operator was saying that the vessel was listing and beginning to tip over as it was full of ice. It was terrible to listen to those kinds of conversations. Our skipper had a younger brother on board the vessel, so when he heard the message, I thought he was going to go berserk. He was shouting and screaming and totally going off his head. As you can imagine, it was a terrible situation for everyone.

We were trying to get to a place called Isafjord in north west Iceland, for shelter, and, like I said earlier, so were lots of other trawlers; it was terrible.

We went down a big passageway and then we had to cross an open area, where the trawlers were dodging around a place called Ritur Hook. That was where the wind would nigh on blow us over.

The skipper turned the vessel around and 'ran ' back out, as we were getting nowhere. With all this manoeuvring, we were still getting iced up, which was putting us in a very unstable condition.

On the map, you will be able to see the route to Isafjord and the open area the trawlers needed to cross to reach the safe haven. So, sad; so close, and yet so far for the stricken ships.

One of the other trawlers, 'Ross Cleveland', had been away from its home port (Hull) for quite a while, so was in a fragile condition. They had consumed a lot of oil and water and not too much fish had gone down into the hold.

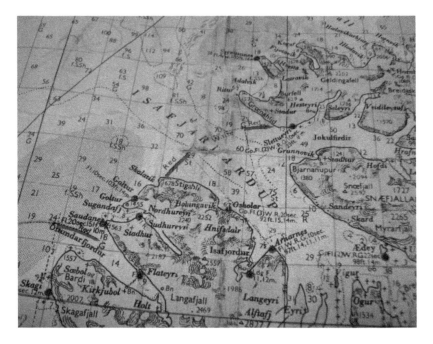

Map of the area.

We and all the other trawlers had to cross this area where the wind was absolutely screeching and could blow us over, but we had to do it to get to calmer waters and shelter.

I was still on the bridge with the skipper and my watch mates, trying to keep the radar reasonably clear to help us navigate down the narrow fjord, (especially as it was dark).

The 'Ross Cleveland' was ahead of us by about a quarter of a mile.

I had just come back on deck after getting a hot mug of tea when I heard something that would stay with me for many years. The skipper on the 'Ross Cleveland', Phil Gay, was talking on the radio.

He was saying, to the surrounding vessels, that they were 'going down' (sinking) and asking for any ships in the area to try to assist them. It was absolutely devastating, the way he was talking. Ironically, according to his position, he was so close to us, but visibility was poor, and our radar was not receiving, so we could not see him.

Phil said to give his wife and family all his love, as well as those of all his crew members. Believe me; it was unbearable to hear this. I was crying and my fellow crew members were also shedding tears.

We did manage to get a small target on our radar which we believed was the 'Ross Cleveland' and, for a few brief moments, we could actually see some faint lights in the distance.

Please remember that the wind was greater than Force 11 and it was snowing constantly. With the black frost as well, conditions were out of this world.

We could hear broken conversations from Icelandic vessels, especially the coastguard of the local ferry that was carrying passengers. It was so terrible; all these conversations and cries for help were on the VHF radios constantly.

The Icelandic gunboat did a marvellous job battling the elements to try and reach sinking vessels and survivors who had frostbite.

We looked on our radar; the small target just disappeared from the screen. So we looked with the naked eye to see if we could see anything of the 'Ross Cleveland' as, between the snow squalls, you could get a blinkering of the vessel's lights, but we saw nothing.

The crew on board the 'Kingston Garnet' were just numb. The atmosphere was awful. No one was speaking, they just sat there with their thoughts; possibly wondering, "Which will be the next ship to go down? Will it be us?"

At that moment, I could see that our skipper was really down, as he was still not sure if his brother's ship was safe or not. Also, we had seen the 'Ross Cleveland' go down with all hands in a matter of minutes. Nevertheless, the skipper forged ahead with his orders, to get us to safety.

Those were the longest 18 hours of my life. I felt so tired and helpless. I had completed my 18 hours' duty, so was relieved and went to the mess room (still fully rigged and on standby, in case I was needed).

I must have fallen asleep, sitting up, as when I was waking up, I thought I was in a dream. The ship was as steady as a rock, as if we were sailing on a swimming pool. It was unbelievable.

I gathered my senses and staggered onto the deck, gazing around in amazement. The sea was flat, and we were going slowly up the fjord, with large mountains on each side of us.

I knew then, that before we went to the jetty, we would have to bring the forward derrick in and do small securing jobs before we got alongside.

During the dark hours and with gale force winds, you tend to just get your head down and get stuck into the job you are assigned to do, so you don't take in too much of the surroundings. In the daylight, when you look around, you can appreciate what has happened.

The ship was nearly a block of ice; never had I seen anything like this before, and neither had the older crew members. All our working wires, which were going to the blocks on the forward mast, were normally about one and a half inches in diameter, but then, covered in ice, I could not even wrap my arms around them. It was incredible!

So there we were, going towards the small Icelandic town of Isafjord. I could see the jetty in the distance, so the deck crew started to down the decks with the 'donkey'; a slang term for the water supply. In this case, it was hot water being supplied to the main deck, so that we could get rid of some of the excess ice before being secured to the jetty.

When we were a few hundred yards from the jetty, the 'local pilot' came out and boarded the ship, guiding the skipper towards the jetty. At this time, I was in the crosstrees at the top of the mast, securing the derrick. I was also watching the ship's track.

We were rounding this bend when, all of a sudden, the ship started leaning over. I thought I was going to fall out! I was thinking, "What else can go wrong for us?" Everything was becoming too much.

The skipper shouted to us all and said not to worry. We had just touched the bottom and would have to wait a couple of hours for the tide to rise a little bit more, than we could continue, which we did.

The pilot and the skipper berthed us alongside the small jetty.

The skipper's intentions were to stay at the dock/jetty and reinstall our radio antennas (they had all been broken or lost in the storm) and get everything in good shape for sailing out, when the weather let us.

It was a big relief as, for days, we had been tossed about, listening to the 'Ross Cleveland' sinking, and I think we, the crew, were traumatised. We hadn't been able to sleep or rest, so alongside the jetty, we knew we could at least catch up on this.

Once we had been secured to the jetty, we saw some other vessels follow us through and secure to the other jetty, further down. As I mentioned earlier, all the ships were in the same predicament as we were. I think there were another four or so trawlers from Hull; maybe two from BUT. We did go on to the other trawlers, to see how the crews were, pay our respects and see if we could help anyone with anything.

There was a strange feeling around; something I couldn't explain, from that day to this. I remember that we rested up on board our ship, then decided to go onshore for a stroll, just to get our legs on 'dry land'. So, as best we could, we got cleaned up, put on fresh clothes and wrapped up well, then set off.

We ended up at a church, and saw other crews doing the same. This, I do believe, was some kind of guidance from the Lord Almighty, as nothing had been arranged between ourselves and the other ships.

We all entered the church, still carrying this strange feeling, and when we got inside, we saw that all the locals had come to pray for their loved ones, children and adults alike, who had been drowned or maimed in the bad weather crisis. The local villages used boats for their main transportation purposes; even getting the children to the main ports for school.

You can imagine how many people had been affected by this storm, which had literally occurred on their doorstep. It was horrific. The church was absolutely packed with young and old alike; everyone moved into their places and, please appreciate the situation; at this time, the Icelandic people were very restricted in the English language, and we didn't speak Icelandic!

The priest was standing nervously near the pulpit, trying to seat everyone; all of whom were terribly upset.

We had one deckhand with us; his name was Doc Holliday and he was a great bloke; nothing was ever too much for him. Well, we all had our 'decent clothes' on and Doc was wearing his denims. He walked up to the pulpit and exchanged a lot of hand signals with the local priest, and next thing we know, Doc is in the pulpit, asking everyone to pray. He was talking and praying, praying and talking, and the sight was one I will never ever forget, as very few people there could speak or understand English, and there was Doc from Hessle Road, praying and talking to the flock.

At that moment, it did not matter what language you spoke. It was amazing, as everyone was on the same level. It was such a moving service.

At the end, all the locals came to us fisherman and tried to say words of comfort. We, in return, were attempting to do the same. Handkerchiefs was everywhere. It was amazing and touching.

After the church service, we fisherman started to stroll back to our ships, to see what the latest news would be regarding the weather conditions 'outside'.

When we arrived back on board our ship, 'Kingston Garnet', I wrote a letter to my wife, to tell her that we were safe, as I was sure the newspapers would be full of all kinds of stories. The letter I sent to my wife can be seen over the next few pages. You will be able to see my thoughts at that time.

I know it must have been horrendous for all the families involved in the fishing industry. It was a complete disaster and, for me, it will never go away. It is always in my mind, re-living the conditions we went through, and not just the ship I was on, but all the vessels in our area. It was absolutely the worst weather conditions I have ever experienced in my full sea-going life.

Even now, as I am writing these incidents down, I still get goose bumps.

Anyhow, we sat down and had our 'tea' and we felt better, as this was basically the first meal we could sit down and enjoy in comfort for 48-72 hours.

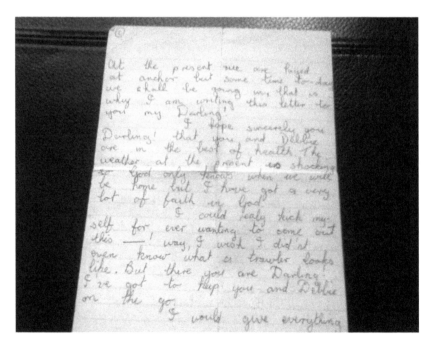

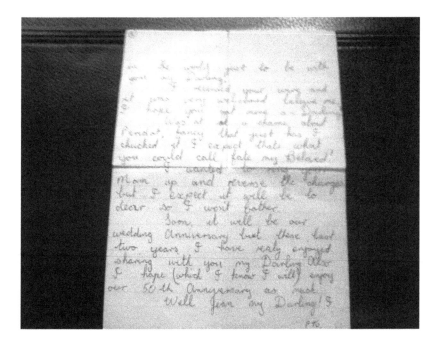

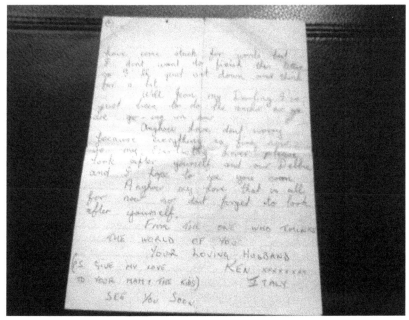

Letter to my wife, Jean, following the triple trawler tragedy.

As you can see, the letter is still in very good condition, even after all these years. Again, the memories all flood back. The rest of the crew also put pen to paper.

It's in this kind of situation that you think someone up there must have been looking down on us and helping us through a very difficult time. When I think back, it was a very saddening experience for all the people involved. Personally, I did not think we were going to lose our lives. I really thought that we would get through it. However, there are times when you doubt yourself and experience thoughts and feelings that are certainly not pleasant. The night in question was so scary and the initial thought was that all the trawlers in the vicinity, as well as the ships in the fjords, would become top heavy with ice and all would be lost; hundreds and maybe thousands of souls in one night. But once those thoughts have flashed through your mind, you have to become more motivated and carry on knocking ice from the ship.

So on that evening, after our crew had de-iced the vessel and 'squared up' the decks, we felt like a good night's rest would not go amiss. We had heard that the other trawlers had been in touch with their respective offices and reached agreements that they would make their ships seaworthy then proceed to their home ports; Grimsby, Hull, Fleetwood or Aberdeen. At this moment in time, we were still not sure what our skipper's intentions were.

At about 7pm, I decided to get some well-deserved sleep and went to my bunk, which was in the focsle (the forward part of the ship). The 'Kingston Garnet' had adequate accommodation, as it slept crew aft and also forward. This meant that only about four spare hands slept forward, which was good, as there was a lot of cupboard space to stow your personal things and we could keep the quarters clean. It was also good as we could sit there and tell each other good sea yarns, make plans and tell each other what we intended to do when we got back home.

Anyhow, like I said, I was dozing off into a nice sleep when one of my shipmates (Mally) came and woke me up. His words were, "Come on, Ken. I think something is going on."

I was by no means the senior deckman/spokesman, but I just thought I would say what I thought was right, as I was just a normal young chap, with a beautiful wife and two babies waiting for me at home. So, for sure I wanted to ask a lot of questions and I wanted answers. It was terrifying to me at times, although I did not show it. It was a strange and dangerous situation to be in. I wanted to speak up for my crewmates, as we had all sailed with each other in the past on various company vessels, and we all knew each other. I really did not want my life to stop at 20 years old, so I become, at that moment, a man to reckoned with. I thought, "I am here for my wife and children and by hell, I will certainly stand up for what I believe is the right thing to do." Please remember that the fishing industry in Hull was a good one to be in if you wanted to better yourself, so I did not want to be classed as an idiot and really was ready for a confrontation with whoever wanted one. I was sticking up for myself and those who agreed with me.

I jumped out of my bunk and Mally and myself went aft to the galley to get a pot of tea. We were pretty close as we were the 'fish room crew'. There were only two people doing that job, and if the two of you got on well, it would make the job a lot easier and quicker. The fish room crew got a 'backhander' from the mate, especially if they turned out a good-quality catch and grossed good money.

So Mally and myself were in the galley, just having a pot of tea, and I could hear the main engine on line, when normally we just had the generator running for lighting etc. When you've just woken up and hear a different noise, you tend to let it go for the time being.

Mally was bringing me up to date with what he had heard and his opinion. By then, there were a few more members of the deck crew coming into the galley.

What happened next takes some believing, but read with interest, as it will never ever escape my thoughts.

We were talking away about things in general, including our thoughts on the skipper's intentions, when we felt like we had bumped against something. Of course, this seemed very strange and was not to be expected, so we ran to the deck to see what the cause was.

While we had been talking, the mate had sneaked along the deck on his own. He had done this on the skipper's orders, of course, but at that time, there were only three people who knew this, and they were the skipper, mate and pilot.

It was dark and very icy, and he released our mooring lines to the shore. So, the skipper, in his wisdom (God bless him) thought he could sneak away, and once we were clear. . . who knows?

So, we were free of our moorings.

I was absolutely devastated and immediately shouted to Mally, "I am jumping to shore, as the skipper is pulling off to sea without the communications being repaired or anything!"

That being said, I stumbled onto the jetty among the piles of snow and ice and, believe me, it was bitter there. Mally immediately followed me and we were both huddled together in this small storage shed doorway on the jetty.

We glanced up at the bridge and saw a 'local pilot'. He was there to guide us out of the channel as we headed towards to sea. I also saw our skipper, and he looked slightly worse for wear !!!

At that moment, the mate saw Mally and me and shouted to us to get on board. I cannot print my answer, but I think you know what I said back! The mate immediately informed the skipper that two crewmembers had jumped ship.

I saw the skipper come out onto the bridge and we made eye contact. He shouted to us, "You two f***ing idiots get back on board now!"

Of course, we shouted back 'naughty' words. The skipper shouted that he would 'log' us and I replied that he could f*** us for all I was bothered, as Mally and I were not going back on that ship until it was secured to the jetty and the engines shut down. Then we would talk.

This situation went on for an hour and Mally and I kept saying to each other that we would stick it out, even though we were getting very cold with the (literally) freezing conditions!

The skipper eventually gave in and instructed the rest of the crew to re-secure the ship alongside the jetty. This was done, the engines were shut down and the 'local pilot' disembarked. The mate had a smug look on his face and I was disgusted by his actions. Basically, he had been prepared to potentially put the lives of 19 men in danger. I just walked past him, treating him with the contempt he deserved.

The skipper called me to his cabin and on his desk, he had the official log nook open. I looked at his face and knew he had been drinking. He tried to put on a sombre expression, but it was not working. He said that, in view of my actions, which were very serious, he had no alternative but to 'log' me. If that happened, I knew I would be blacklisted and, even worse, may not be able to return to sea for a lengthy period of time.

I also knew that the skipper was slightly intoxicated, and that I had to stand my ground.

He was quoting from the contents of the log book, including the word 'mutiny', which was making me very uneasy. Bearing in mind that in this situation there really was no 'freedom of speech' or HSE (Health, Safety and Environment) so I knew I had to present a strong case.

The skipper then started telling me he was going to 'log' me and that I would not be able to return to sea, as my actions would be classed as a serious case of mutiny.

I was starting to become upset and angry, so I blurted out my argument. I told the skipper that he had promised us we would stay at the jetty and carry out our repairs before discussing our next plan. I told him that we would work our hands off for him and anything he needed, we would be behind him 100 per cent, but only on the understanding that the repairs be carried out prior to departure.

I could see and feel the skipper easing off a little. He then said to me, "OK, Ken. Let's forget the log book." I also got an apology from him, about being worse for wear.

The sad thing about the skipper's actions is that I do believe he was fuelled by the mate's attitude. He was giving the skipper false support. I truly understood why he had been intoxicated, what with everything that had happened to ourselves and the surrounding ships, plus the all-night ordeal. He may have been thinking that his younger brother had been lost. These were the things that had been on his mind, but now that they were getting sorted out, I believed he was mellowing a bit.

Well, the skipper went on to outline his plan, which was to get all the communication problems (broken antennas etc.) sorted out before sailing. He then called a general meeting with the crew to inform them of his intentions and ask if anyone had any objections to sailing the ship to the south east part of Iceland (where it was, hopefully, warmer and there were better sea conditions). There, he would try to catch more fish, which would mean a better financial return for the crew.

So we discussed the situation and everyone agreed, so that would be the plan.

At that moment, I was not too impressed with the mate, as something wasn't ringing quite right. I could not put my finger on it, but there was something.

There were some trawler trips where you would have to call into a foreign port, whether for technical or medical reasons, so I would take this opportunity to write to Jeannie, just to let her know how things were doing, even though sometimes I would arrive home before the letter did, ha ha! In those days, no one really thought about letters, so my way was a little old-fashioned, but I would get a piece of paper from the radio operator, create a makeshift envelope, then stick the sides together with jam or treacle!

So the following day, when all was repaired and tested, we set sail for the south east of Iceland, which would take us about 36 hours. Everything had been secured on deck i.e. trawl and all the relevant equipment and tools. There was still a big covering of ice/snow on the deck, but it was not affecting our stability, and hopefully, the further south we went, the warmer the weather, to defrost the ice. Also, please remember that we were the only trawler to steam back onto the fishing grounds, as the other trawlers had decided to steam directly to their home ports.

So away we went down to the south east of Iceland. We shot our nets away at a place called Whaleback and the weather was fresh. There was a strong breeze blowing, but in relation to the weather we had just been through, it was nothing.

We towed the gear for about three hours, and in this time, we got all the decks squared away and ship-shape for the catch.

When we were hauling the nets, what we saw was out of this world! I will always remember, as it was about 3am and dark. As we were pulling in the top part of the trawl, the cod ends and the bellies came rushing up to the surface.

The skipper had got us a very large catch. It was music to our ears!

We brought the fish on board and the crew then became more pleasant, as we knew this would heal the wounds from earlier on in the voyage.

We filled the starboard side and part of the port side, then the skipper shouted to us all to keep the trawl inboard for the time being, until we had got so much of the fish below decks, just in case the weather broke. Which, of course, I would say was a good decision, as we could also keep the fish in good condition. Then, when the decks were clearer, we could shoot the trawl again.

I was the fish room man, so me, Mally and the deckie learner dropped down the hatch and started putting the fish into the holding sections (known as pounds). Then, not long afterwards, I could hear the skipper shouting out something, but I couldn't make out what it was.

The bosun (Brian Lilley) shouted down to us to come up on deck, which we did immediately. I think the skipper had just lost it, as he was screaming, "Swill the fish away!" and kept repeating the same message. So, we had to obey his command and started to swill the good fish back into the sea.

At that moment in time, I could not believe what I was hearing. After everything we had been through, this catch was part of our financial recovery. It really did seem like madness!

During this operation, I was relieved by one of my shipmates, so went to my bunk to get my six hours' rest before starting my next 18 hours.

I fell asleep immediately, and when I awoke, the trawler seemed as steady as a rock. So, I went out on deck and saw that we were steaming into a port called Seydisfjord. Believe me, I was so shocked; I didn't know what to say! Then I saw the mate, on the bridge. He came down and told me that the skipper had (or was beginning to have) a nervous breakdown. This really upset me, as the skipper had tried his very best for his crew and ship. Regardless of our disagreement in Isafjord, I would have worked around the clock for him, and I did. I still hold very high respect and regard for him.

We moored up alongside and watched an ambulance come and take our skipper away. The ambulance crew were talking to him quietly, and the skipper was just in a daze.

About an hour later, after the mate had been ashore with the agent, he returned and called all the crew into the mess room. The mate then told us about the situation. He said he had spoken to the owners and also the insurance company and had received special permission to bring the 'Kingston Garnet' back to Hull as soon as possible.

Personally, I did not rate the mate, but maybe I was being a bit nasty, as I thought very highly of our skipper, and the mate seemed to be acting very immaturely.

When we got underway the first time, the vessel rolled somewhat and took water on board. Straight away, the mate eased the speed down, which told me he was nervous. This didn't help him command our respect.

Well, again we secured the ship's decks, got the pilot on board and sailed for sea.

It was four days later that we entered the River Humber, and for all of us on board, it was a very reassuring sight to see.

The next day, we landed our fish and got paid our poundage. The money was sufficient, but we should have been given a lot more, after what we had been through; especially when I picture the amount of fish on our decks that we swilled away. But some you win and some you lose.

The 'Kingston Garnet' was kept in the dock for a number of days, so that was good for me (and the rest of the crew). We could spend some prime time with our loved ones. I tried to shut myself away from what we had all just been through.

After a week, I was told to go down to the fish dock and sign back on the articles for sailing on the 'Kingston Garnet'. I asked the office who the new skipper was, and when I was told. . . well I nearly fell over, as this man's name was not well-regarded, to say the least! I had heard stories of how badly he treated the crews.

So again, we left the Hull fish dock and started steaming towards Iceland. All the crew members were very nervous, firstly, because of the new skipper on board and the stories we had heard, and secondly, we were proceeding to Iceland; hoping we would not be going back to the North Cape area, where we encountered all the bad weather and misfortunes.

All I can say is, "It never rains but it pours." Yes, the new skipper was intent on taking us to just about the exact spot where we had experienced all the bad weather on the previous trip.

The bosun, Brian, a good friend and shipmate, was getting edgy about us going to the North Cape of Iceland again. Brian was a very good, reliable shipmate and for him to get nervous was not a good sign.

When we arrived on the fishing grounds, the weather was good, so that was a bonus, but unfortunately, Brian would not come out on deck. The skipper called down to me (he knew Brian and I were shipmates) and asked me to go and see what the problem was.

I went to the bosun's cabin and Brian was in there with all his deck gear on, just sitting there, muttering to himself. It was terrible for me to see him like that. I said, "Come on, Brian. Let's get going," but he was just in a different world, muttering away about things. I could not even understand him. I tried to coax him out, but it was a waste of time.

Then the skipper came in, looked at Brian, and returned to the bridge.

When I went back on deck, the skipper called me to the bridge and said he had no choice but to send Brian to shore for medical treatment, which I knew was the best thing to do. There was no way Brian could stay with us, as not only would he be a danger to the crew, but also to himself. Brian Lilley deserved better than that as, to me, he was a stalwart of the industry; a forgotten hero. Brian will stay with me forever.

So this was the after-effect of the trip before. I was beginning to wonder if I would become a victim, and when!

We went into the Icelandic port and the bosun was put ashore, then we sailed, shorthanded, back to the fishing grounds. Thank God the trip passed without any incidents and all was OK.

We got back and settled our wages and I signed off the 'Kingston Garnet' as, by this time, I believed I was worthy of a better vessel.

Brian Lilley stayed onshore for some time, for medical reasons. The skipper, I am sorry to say, passed away at sea on board the 'Kingston Onyx' on the 8th February 1969. I believe he was 47 years old.

I must put in this piece as, one time when I was out of a ship (on unemployment benefit/dole) I got a job at our local chocolate factory, called Needlers. At this time, we were living down Fountain Road in a two-up two-down. Small, nevertheless nice, happy and clean.

Well, at this factory I worked my heart out, pushing big trolleys full of all kinds of things, and it was really tiring! At the end of the second week (I had to work a week in hand) the size of my wage was just about nothing. I told my boss that this wage was not good for me, as I was a married man with a family. He immediately told me it was because I was under 21. I told him where to put the job and he was not too impressed! I walked home merrily, knowing that very soon I would be on the high seas once more.

A few days later, I then signed on a trawler called 'Kingston Emerald', which was a lot newer and bigger than the 'Kingston Garnet', so I felt very good about myself. The skipper's name was Brian Boyce and he was just starting his career as skipper. This was his biggest ship so far and he was going to do well; this was his chance to shine.

'Kingston Emerald' in 'Kingston colours'.
(Skippers: Brian Boyce and Dave Grewar).

I ended up staying with the 'Kingston Emerald' for one year, then they kept her in dock for a 'Lloyds survey', which was to take three months.

While on board the 'Kingston Emerald', we had some good times. The crew were all good shipmates and the skipper was good, too. He fished in bad weather, but it was worth it, as slowly the ship was moving up in 'The Challenge Shield', where trawlers would compete against each other for one year to see who would win this shield. Of course, if you were in a big trawler, a newish one, and had a good skipper, well you were in with a good chance! Also, the trawler would expect to do a decent speed.

Skippers took one or maybe two trips off for holiday, so it was always interesting to see who would come to relieve the regular skipper.

One time, when skipper Brian Boyce was having a couple of trips off, we had a chap called Dave Grewar. (I hope you will all remember these names, as our paths will cross again sometime before the ending of the book). Anyhow, Dave Grewar was a Ross's man, and, if I speak the truth, there was a bit of 'leg-pulling' and gentle rivalry, so of course, when the new skipper arrived on board, he was going to do all sorts and break all kinds of financial records. (We had heard this story a few times previously!).

So we sailed back to our second home; glorious Iceland! The first trip went by OK, A normal trip; again, no big records broken, no accidents (that was good) so all was fine. Dave came back for one more trip and again we went to south east Iceland and that was the trip; we did it! We filled the ship up. The total catch, if I remember rightly, was 3200 kits. I was down in the fish room, and in all the time I had spent on the 'Kingston Emerald', we had never got this far, regarding filling up the fish room. For me, it was great, as I felt good and I knew we had done a good job looking after the fish, as the mate gave the fish room squad a good backhander (financial gift).

So, we were full up and left for home! (Also the market prices were good, so we had a really good trip and were all very pleased).

The normal thing was for all the crew (or at least the majority) to get together for maybe one night while we were at home, and just have a drink together. Our jobs were dangerous, difficult and demanding, so we had earned our little get-togethers when we were home.

So that's how it was on board the 'Kingston Emerald'. As she was in contention for winning 'The Challenge Shield', we did work hard, but we also got some good earnings from the 'Kingston Emerald'.

There was one spare hand called Danny Mcloughlin. He was originally from Fleetwood, but he was a good old stick. Danny had been on the 'Kingston Sapphire'; one of four vessels similar to the 'Kingston Emerald'.

It was the year 1968 (November) and my wife had just given birth to a beautiful baby girl. She named her Lisa Marie, which was a coincidence, as that was when Elvis Presley's daughter was born with the same name.

Danny was spare hand with us and didn't have a clue that he was on board the 'Kingston Emerald' as opposed to his regular ship, the 'Kingston Sapphire'. He was, (what can I say?) intoxicated for five days, which may be an understatement, but Danny, God bless him, was a really good shipmate. Yes, five days it took Danny to realise, but when we got back to St Andrew's Dock, he had a good settling to pick up, so he was very happy about that.

It was such a shame for the Hull fisherman, as we were classed as 'casual labour'. It was just another excuse for the owners not to have to pay us any money if, for some reason, we became out of work. So, if your ship was having a survey, you had the right to claim dole. It was very little money, but again, better than nothing.

Of course, I was out of work sometimes and the system in those days was that you could 'sign on' the unemployment register, which entitled you to unemployment benefit. So I went ahead and signed on the dole (this was while the 'Kingston Emerald' was having the 'Lloyd Survey') and did receive a small amount from the government.

After a few weeks, I began to get an itch for the sea again, and at that time, my father was working for Humber Conservancy Board, which, eventually was taken over by British Docks. My father was engaged as first mate on the vessel 'Humber Guardian'. He did this when he wasn't working at his primary job, as master of the 'Bull Light Vessel', which was moored towards the mouth of the River Humber.

Anyhow, the 'Humber Guardian' was a dedicated vessel for maintaining the River Humber's buoyage system. For example, the ship would patrol the river, which was a long and very treacherous one, to make sure all the channel buoys were in operation to assist the vessels when navigating the River Humber.

My father asked me if I would like a try at this job, and I said "yes" so he arranged for an interview with the Humber Conservancy Board. It went well; they told me I would have to do two weeks on the lightship 'Spurn', which was on station at the mouth of the River Humber.

I arrived on board the lightship and there was only one other crewman there. Believe me, it was very strange, as I had been used to getting washed up and down a trawler's deck in high latitudes in the Arctic Circle, and here I was, on an anchored lightship. If another vessel was going to collide with us, we wouldn't stand a chance.

I took loaves of bread and some canned items, on my father's advice, as we cooked our own food on board. Regarding my cooking ability, at that time of my life, it wasn't good! The only thing I knew about food was how to eat it! In terms of preparation, I didn't have a clue, so for two weeks, I lived on chips, toast and beans and the odd fish, when I could get my fishing line out.

I struggled through those two weeks and realised that that kind of job was not for me, as it was too boring, and, at times, the conversation was repetitive. I was glad to go home.

Buoy maintenance vessel, 'Humber Guardian'.

After one week of being at home, I was assigned to the 'Humber Guardian' as deckhand and I was pleased. At that time, my mode of transport was bicycle, which was good for me, as sometimes I would have to be on board between 2 and 3am. This was dependent on the tides, as the ship could only sail at high water, or thereabouts.

The job was very interesting, especially with my father as first mate! It made me feel good.

After a few weeks, I was getting called to the ship at unsociable hours. I remember one day, I had slept in, then jumped on my bike and it had a flat tyre, so I had to repair it before I set off for the docks. I arrived at the dockside late and the 'Humber Guardian' had already departed, as the tide was starting to fall, and the captain said he would wait for me just off the dock.

When I arrived, there was a small boat waiting to take me to the 'Humber Guardian'. I asked one of the crew to take my bike and they refused, so I just told them, "If my bike does not go, I will not go either!" and, needless, to say they took my bike.

When I boarded the 'Humber Guardian', the captain was not a happy man! He told me that I was losing myself a lot of overtime, not being on time for work.

I saw my father looking a bit disappointed, so I apologised, then work resumed.

I must admit, the captain did commend me on my work. I will also state that before I joined the 'Humber Guardian', the crew had been receiving 'short hand money', meaning that, if a crew member is missing, the working crew share that person's money between them. Of course, I was the missing man, and when I did start work, the 'short hand money' stopped, so the crew members were not too happy about that situation.

I can say, hand on heart, I was never lazy, would always do my part and would also help others whenever I could.

Anyhow, when we got to port later in the day, I spoke to my father and explained that it would be better for me to leave the 'Humber Guardian' rather than keep putting my father in a difficult situation. He asked what I would do for work, and I told him that the 'Kingston Emerald' had just about finished her survey, so I would return to her.

So away I went, back down to the fish dock.

It is very hard to explain the feeling of being pulled back to sea; back to the adventure, the danger. Whatever it was, it kept pulling me back.

Everything was fine, as I was entitled to go back to the 'Kingston Emerald', as one of the original crew.

When we got on board for sailing, the ship was a complete mess! It smelt of new paint and there was rubbish thrown everywhere. I know lots of people think that fishermen are untidy, but that's incorrect! We were on our sea home, and we had respect for our living environment.

Anyhow, we sailed to Iceland and the skipper did well for himself and all his crew; we were earning good money. The money was well-deserved, though, as the skipper would fish in all weather conditions. Things were going well. . . then word started going around that there could be a possible strike in the trawlers.

Trawlermen were very hardy and would work for days on end if need be, so we were all wondering what was happening. At this time, I was about 20 years old, so still only a baby. However, I had a nice wife and family.

When I think back, the forthcoming strike was about wages, and I thought it would be good if we could achieve more.

Well, the days passed, and the talk was really strong. Solidarity was difficult to achieve, though, as the trawlers were never all in the port at the same time.

Needless to say, we did go on strike; if that is what you want to call it! Everything started off nice and normally. There were peaceful demonstrations; we used to stand on the dock issuing our protests as our union TWGU instructed us to do. Of course, as time went by, you got the odd one or two who thought they were Superman and made a mess of things.

I would go on 'picket duty' i.e. going down to the dock (whatever time of day and night) to make our presence known.

As the strike was going on, the owners decided to get a group of people to man the trawlers and put 'nice skippers' on board as temptation.

It got so bad that the owners were hiring horse vans to transport the strike breakers through the picket lines. It was getting out of hand! (The men trying to break the strike were called 'scabs'). I do realise that people needed to make a living, but the people who were going on board the trawlers. . . well, some of them had never been to sea before and a lot of the others had been run off in the past, as they were troublemakers. So yes, things got very heated at times

Me and a shipmate, Ron Simister, would go with the taxi driver to pick up these strike breakers and try to persuade them not to sail. So, when getting onto the fish dock, we took them into the union office, which was based on the dock, and the union official would talk them through the reasons for not going. It worked well.

This went on for quite a while, and then we heard that the owners had agreed to the pay increase! This was good news, as we all wanted to get back to sea and start earning our living. While on strike, we had been receiving just five pounds as 'strike pay', which was ridiculous!

Then the union dropped a bombshell. They were very cocky and said, "No, we are staying out until we get one hundred per cent union," which was madness! Then things started to get worse. Lots of aggression was shown and fights broke out.

Eventually, we decided to get back to sea. I had been home a long time; officially, the fisherman's strike began 12th February 1970, and lasted nine weeks. I got barely anything out of the deal; it was terrible.

Months later, there was still lots of resentment, if you found out that some of your shipmates had been strike breakers.

'Lord Ancaster'. (Skipper Dave Atkinson).

I was on the trawler 'Lord Ancaster' with a skipper called Dave Atkinson, and the trip was not too bad, except the skipper was a 'bit strange' to say the least! Anyhow, he gave me this particular job, which meant lifting the floor from the bridge and getting down to the bottom of the bridge floor. The depth was about another 4ft. He told me to clean, brush, then paint the area. Such jobs were usually dealt with by the shore people, once the ship was back in dock.

The conversation got out of control and some heated words were exchanged! Anyhow, I thought, at the end of my watch (I was spare hand and we were steaming home) that it was all ok. We were due to be docking that day in the fish dock at Hull, and when we got to the entrance of the River Humber, the dock master told our skipper to keep coming, and we would just get into the dock, as it would be 'top of tide'. When we make our approach to the jetty, the normal way is stern first, but the high tide would soon start to ebb, and time was important. We knew we could always swing the ship around when we got through the lock pits into the dock.

I was on the foredeck and we had got all the mooring ropes prepared for going alongside. I was walking aft when I heard the bosun shout to everyone, "Hang on!" I grabbed the handrail and turned my body around. I saw us still going forward, towards Barton Rope Company jetty. Well. . . we ran through the jetty and just stopped near the fence.

Everything was made of wood, so that was good, as cement would have probably dented the bow; maybe even cracked it!

So when all had settled down, we managed to get back alongside the jetty. We edged our way into the fish dock, swung around and berthed up at the fish market for offloading the following day.

The skipper was at fault, regarding the collision, as insurance states that, before entering the River Humber, the vessel should be stopped and engines put into astern/reverse mode. The skipper didn't do this, so he was banned from sailing as skipper for one year.

The next day, I went down to the fish dock to settle up. I was in a good mood. I took my wife's uncle with me. He was called Maurice and he lived in Fleetwood. He and his wife were in Hull, visiting my wife's mother, so Maurice and I talked about the trip and it was good to have him with me.

There I was, full of confidence and feeling good, but when I walked into the office, the ship's runner said to me, "What have you been doing?" I thought he was joking and said, "What do you mean?"

It turns out that the skipper had suddenly sacked me! Not only that, but he entered in my seaman's/discharge book a 'vg' (very good) for work but a 'mod' (moderate) for ability! I was like a mad dog, as up to then, I had never been sacked, and for this to be in my seaman's book was absolutely unacceptable. I was raging.

People were telling me to calm down and I cannot repeat what I said back to them! Straight away, I went upstairs to the cashier and settled my wages, then I went back downstairs and onto the dockside, waiting for a confrontation with this skipper who had been childish and destroyed my feelings about him.

Patience is a virtue and, finally, he came strolling into the office with a big cigar hanging out of his mouth! He said, "Good morning, Ken" and "Good trip" and all minor chitchat. I immediately said, "What's this about the discharge?" He was flabbergasted and did not know what to say, so I really told him what I thought of him!

He said, "Ken, it wasn't me! It must have been the mate!" (who I also did not like, as I had sailed with him on the 'Kingston Garnet').

Anyhow, luck was on my side as the mate came walking up, so I got them both arguing between themselves while Maurice and I just walked away in disgust, to have a drink at Rayners Bar!

The next day, I was still raging, so I went down to the dock and got my book from the ship's runner. I said I would go to insurance and get it cancelled from my book. The people in the office looked at me if I was had just come out from under a rock!

I told them that the fishing industry had been run on corruption and 'jobs for the boys', but that the new generation (which I was a part of) would get it all changed for the better.

Men would get a job on their merit, not because they were friends of the skipper or mate, or even slipped the ship's runner some money.

The setup really angered me.

I arrived at the insurance buildings on the dock and had a meeting with the ex-master, who was good, fair and precise. I told him exactly what had happened, and he looked into my seafaring history and told me he would handle it. He said to return in a day or so.

On my return, the ex-master was true to his word; 'mod' had been changed to 'vg and satisfactory', which was great.

When I went back to my office to tell them what happened at the insurance buildings, they seemed to look down at me. I thought, "Just let me get the mate or skipper, then we will see who is correct."

Yes. . . you could say I was a man on a mission.

Stern trawler 'Othello'. (Skipper Neville Beevers).

Why I had supposedly been a 'bad boy', I will never know.

I signed on the stern freezer, 'Othello', with a skipper called Neville Beevers. It's strange how things go. . . when I was a small boy, my family lived on the same street as Neville!

We sailed and, again, please remember that during my fishing career, the longest time I had been on a trawler for was 26 days (apart from when I was on 'St Alcuin') and I would be on the 'Othello' for 12 weeks or so.

My family and I were going to be apart a long time.

I did the trip (this was October 1970) and when I got home, I decided I wanted to be back on the 'old sidewinders', as I missed this a lot.

Again, I found my way back on board the lucky 'Kingston Emerald', where I did a further two trips, then I moved across to the 'Lord St Vincent'; a smaller ship, but a lot newer. Unfortunately, she could not compete with the 'big boys', but, nevertheless, we did earn some good money.

'Lord St Vincent'. (Skipper George Drewery).

So, life went on; the strike became history. The year was 1971 and I started my climb up the ladder again, signing on as third hand/bosun's assistant. I was in charge of a watch, as an unofficial officer, and I really enjoyed it.

'Kingston Amber' (Skipper Mal Clarke).

I signed on the 'Kingston Amber' and we did a 23-day trip to the White Sea which, for me, was a pleasure. I had spent most of my time near Iceland, where the weather was always bad, so the White Sea was a good experience for me and I enjoyed it.

I was only relieving another crew member on the 'Kingston Amber', so after two trips, I was signed off and the permanent third hand came back. For the record, the skipper was called Mal Clark and the mate was the skipper's brother-in-law, Wally Atkinson. For some reason, Wally and myself never got on. Don't get me wrong, Wally was a first-class mate and knew his job through and through, but we just never hit it off. The story does not stop here, because I signed off the ship and later on in this book, Wally and myself will cross paths once more !

I did a couple more trips, then decided to go to school for my bosun's ticket. I was at school for approximately six weeks, learning to net, mend the difficult parts of the trawl, prepare to be an officer and leader and learn the 'rules of the road'. Yes, this was another step up the ladder.

Up to this point, I felt I had travelled a long and bumpy road and was really hoping I was on the verge of moving off the bottom rungs of the ladder.

Chapter 6

BOSUN

Once I had completed my bosun studies, I had to go to the fish dock to the insurance buildings, where ex-skippers/captains would examine my ability and knowledge. I passed and, proud as punch, went to report to the company ship's husband. (The ship's husband was in charge of seeing people like mates and skippers and had some influence over the manager, so it was good to be friends with any ship's husband).

I signed on as spare hand on board the 'Lord St Vincent', which was a smaller vessel, but a lot newer. I did three trips and the skipper told me that I could relieve the regular bosun, which was fine with me! I did the two trips relieving, then I signed off, as the office told me that they would give me a 'regular' bosun's job.

The office signed me on as bosun on an old trawler called the 'Kingston Almandine', which was fine, as I knew I had to start somewhere!

I was pretty nervous when I went on board. I knew the skipper, as I had been deckie learner with him a few years earlier, when he was mate on the 'St Matthew', so that was some consolation. The mate was a much older man, and it turned out he was not a good man to know.

'Kingston Almandine'.
(Skippers: Terry Poskitt and Charlie Andrews).

It was a youngish crew and the men needed some leadership. The mate was not the one to give them this, as he was as bad as they were. He was with them in their cabins, drinking heavily. I issued threats to get them on deck and it did the trick, but I could see I was in for a rough time; especially with it being my first trip as a bosun.

We sailed and when we got close to Iceland, we had to go to a port called Seydisfjord, as we had engine problems.

Well, we got alongside and also alongside was a trawler from Grimsby, and their crew came on board.

It was good to catch up on some well-earned rest, but it wasn't for long.

I heard shouting going on in the mess room, so I went up and, true to form, the mate was drunk as anything and causing trouble; not only with our crew but the lads from the Grimsby trawler. It was absolutely ridiculous! I got in between them and calmed it down a bit.

Then I thought, "Go to bed, Ken, and see what happens tomorrow."

The next day came and we sailed. The skipper said that if I'd had my mate's ticket, he would have left the mate onshore and given me the job, but this was not to be.

When I approached the mate about his part in the ruckus, all he would say is, "I cannot remember", which suited him down to the ground.

Well, after one trip, the mate was fired and we got a new mate. His name was Billy Collins. He was younger and very eager, so things were looking up!

On 20th January 1972, I got a message from my wife via telegram, to say that we were the proud parents of a baby boy! It seemed my little family was complete; a beautiful wife and three beautiful babies. I was over the moon about the news.

Photo of my three children, 1985.

We did a couple of trips to the Norwegian Coast, then back to our stomping ground in good old Iceland (I was destined to do all my sea time at Iceland).

In 1972, discussions were in force regarding the closing down of St Andrews Dock. On November 3rd, 1975, St Andrews Dock was officially closed to shipping.

Albert Dock became the fish dock until the early 1980s, when the trawling industry just disappeared from Hull. Since then, no fishing vessel has ever landed any fish at Albert Dock (to the best of my knowledge). I am led to understand that there may be one vessel, 'Kirkella', which is a freezer vessel, so I would imagine she could land her catch in frozen blocks at any commercial dock.

For approximately three trips, we had a skipper called Charlie Andrews, and he was nicknamed 'Cheque book Charlie'. I do not know for sure, but I think the reason is obvious. With skipper Andrews, we had some experience regarding the 'Cod War'. It was not too bad, but we were told to do as much as possible to stop the Icelandic gunboat crews from boarding the ship. So, before we left Hull Fish Dock, the company gave us lots of lengths of wood, which we shaped into sharp points at one end. Then we inserted these wooden spikes through the scuppers, causing any zodiac boat which approached us to be damaged or even turned over.

This was the beginning of the Cod War at Iceland, and who knew what was round the next corner?

During my trips as bosun, of course the thought passed through me that I would really like to be mate. But as I was still wet behind the ears, I knew it would be a while.

Well, back to reality, and I was on the old 'Kingston Almandine', working as bosun.

The truth is that the older the ship, the less experienced the crew, so sometimes you would really suffer.

I have a sad memory from my time as bosun on the 'Kingston Almandine'. We were fishing at south east Iceland and things were normal. We had a bit of a catch on board; we would not be millionaires, but our families would not starve. Like I said previously, on this class of trawler, the crews were less experienced. (I appreciate that we all have to learn sometime).

One day, as we were hauling, there was a problem with the backstrap on the fore door, so I went along to sort it, as the mate was at the winch.

Afterwards, as I was moving aft to get back to my station, I heard this horrific scream. It came from a young spare hand, and when I looked around, he was just hanging by his arm in the warp top sheave; his hand trapped. It was terrible.

I ran forward, jumping over the fish boards, and got to him first. I screamed at the mate to lower the winch, then wrapped my arms around the lad's legs and lowered him to the deck. It was so hard, seeing how much this young lad of 20 years was hurting. His name was Neil Atkinson and I had sailed with his brother, father and uncle.

I took my knife and cut away his protective clothing, as there was blood dripping from his arm. When I got his outer clothing off, it seemed as if a strange power had taken hold of his hand and twisted and twisted his arm around. It was just like a corkscrew; it was terrible.

Like I said previously, we were fishing at south east Iceland, so the nearest place was a small port in Iceland. Instead, the skipper decided to take the lad to Faroe Island, which was at least 12 hours away. I personally thought this was appalling.

We arrived 14 hours later, in a place called Torshavn. Straight away, the local doctors rushed my shipmate to the hospital.

Straight afterwards, we let the ropes go and proceeded to sea.

We got outside the Faroe fishing limits and again we shot the trawl. We caught some more fish, but nothing like the amount we had been catching at Iceland, so the skipper really let us down by keeping the deckhand in pain and bringing him all the way down to Faroe Island instead of taking him into Iceland.

I did see the deckhand later on. He received all his pay from the trip and was doing well; although it would be a long time before he was back on a trawler.

Normally, if someone gets put ashore for whatever reason, the remaining crew have the right to claim short hand money, but this never happened, as the only time you would claim short hand money was if the man who went to shore was a troublemaker and you wanted to put in a claim. Our shipmate was a good lad for sure.

By this time, I had done six to eight trips as bosun on the 'Kingston Almandine' and was desperate to get off this old ship and onto a better one! Don't get me wrong; I was really thankful to have had my bosun's start on this ship, but now was the time to be moving onwards and upwards.

I signed off the 'Kingston Almandine' and had a few weeks' rest at home, which was good. Then I received a call from the office (BUT) to go down to the dock. When I arrived, I was told I would be signing on as bosun on the 'Kingston Emerald', with skipper Brian Boyce. Firstly, the ship was good and sturdy. Secondly, she was newer than the 'Kingston Almandine', so that was a good thing! I had also sailed with the skipper previously, on the 'Kingston Emerald', and he was good.

However, this was the first time I had been bosun with him, so I was a bit nervous and hopeful that I would do a good job! I was relieving the regular bosun, who was having two trips off for holidays. Yes, I was happy with this situation.

So, we sailed on the 'Kingston Emerald' to Iceland, and if the skipper was a good earner, you tended to get a good, stable, experienced crew, which I knew would make my job a lot easier! Besides, I knew the majority of the crew.

Of course, the skipper lived up to his word and we did a three-week trip with a good catch on board. The work was reasonably easy, and when I settled the next day, I picked up a fair amount, so yes, it was a good experience, being bosun on the 'Kingston Emerald' with skipper Brian Boyce.

The following trip was also a good earner for all on board, but it was coming to an end; I knew I would be signing off to allow back the regular bosun. I had managed to secure two trips with good results, so that was fine for me.

So, at the end of the trip, I signed off, but the next news kind of took the wind out of my sails!

I went down to the dock the day after we arrived in Hull to settle up etc. and was told to go upstairs (which was unheard of) and see the manager, Mr George Hartley. Yes, I had heard of him, and, once or twice, when I had been on the fish market to collect my fish, I had seen him, but we had sort of nodded a casual "Good morning" and nothing else.

MATE

So here I was, in the year 1973, going to have a 'talk with Mr Hartley'. What about? I could never have guessed.

Well, there I was, knocking on the door, and a gruff "Come in" greeted me. I went in and sat down and he asked me if I liked working for BUT etc. Of course, I gave him the answers he wanted to hear.

Straight away he said to me, "Shakesby, I am sending you to school to get your mate's ticket as I believe you will be an asset to the company."

Well, I felt really pleased! This situation happened rarely; a company sending you to school!

So, George Hartley laid out his plans and intentions to me and they seemed very good! In fact, I was a bit lost for words!

That was the meeting sorted out, and I just could not get home quickly enough to tell Jean!

Finally, I got home, and my wife and I spoke about my potential future. It sounded so good! We had a good talk and Jean was very supportive, which I knew she would be.

So, school was sorted out; the start date and duration. If I remember rightly, it was for a period of 13-14 weeks, and as I'd recently completed by bosun's course, I was feeling ok.

So, we started planning for the mate's licence. I had to make sure I had all the materials I needed. The weekly wage we would receive would be just enough to scramble by with, if we were careful, plus we had a little bit of money in the bank, so we would manage alright.

At this time of my life, I was 26 years old, with a beautiful wife and three beautiful children, so I was feeling a bit nervous, but the adrenalin was starting to flow and I felt good in myself.

When I enrolled at school (Hull University College), first and foremost, I saw that the class teacher who helped me with my bosun's ticket was still at college, and he would help me with my mate's licence. His name was Jim Muggeridge; he was a gentleman and a scholar. A really good man. I felt good, as I knew a lot of the lads in my class, and anyone I didn't know personally, I had certainly seen in the pub or down the dock.

So school started and time went by. We were studying all aspects of the 'sea dictionary'. I used to do a lot of homework, once we had all had our tea and I had helped my wife bathe the children and put them to bed.

Jean would help me with the 'semaphore system' (a signalling system). In fact, I do believe my wife got to know the signals better than I did! She would also ask me questions once the children were in bed.

The fishing owners sent the whole class down to a place in Wiltshire called 'HMS Royal Arthur'. This was an onshore naval base but run as if we were on board and at sea. The majority of people there were sitting their chief petty officer rank, so there were quite a few sailors there and we got friendly with them. swapping stories etc.

Each week at the base, there would be a certain exercise put to all the teams of sailors. It was similar to an obstacle race, only much harder, and you ran against the clock.

One weekend, we watched one of the teams doing the race and its name was 'Cliff and Chasm'. The sailors adapted the name to

'Cough and Spasm', so we knew this was going to be good and challenging!

The race went as follows: teams of six persons pulled a handcart, inside of which were two poles with ropes etc. and a barrel weighing 28 pounds.

The object of the exercise was to run downhill with the hand cart, from inside the naval base, then stop the cart, rig up the two spars and, with block and tackle, pull the barrow plus the contents over the 'Chasm'. Then the six members had to get to the other side, rig down and put everything back into the handcart, before running back uphill into the camp and over the finishing line! That's all! Sounds easy!

If I remember rightly, the course record was round about nine minutes, which would take some beating!

No more to be said, we asked our leader (lieutenant) to book us on the course. Everyone said we were crazy and shouldn't be volunteering for this!

For this particular event, all the camp's leaders have to be present i.e. captain, camp doctors and so on.

The next day, we were at the starting line; just the six of us. 'Bang' goes the gun and we are off!

We were pulling the handcart, running downhill, and I thought that the handcart might pass us! We were certainly on a buzz, going down the hill on the first stretch of the course.

I will never forget the way we drove that cart through that event; it was really good!

Then we got the spars rigged and blocks and tackle up and pulled the cart and the barrel of cement over the chasm, before loading everything back into the cart and running back to the finishing line.

We were now going uphill and we really felt it! I thought my legs had locked on me, then in the background, we could hear all the sailors/officers from the camp shouting, "come on you Hull fishermen!"

When we got to the crest, we saw all the people shouting and waving, pushing us on, and it was such a good feeling.

We staggered (and I mean staggered) across the finishing line and once over, we just fell into a heap of under–exercised people! Our course leader, the lieutenant, shouted, "Come on chaps, on yer feet!" Our response cannot be printed; we just laid there until all of our breathing systems were functioning properly.

We got to our feet amidst all the shouting and goings-on, then we found out, officially, that we had been 15 seconds outside the camp record! For us Hull lads, that was amazing! We felt as if we had won a medal for our country! All the ratings, officers, everyone praised us so much; it was really good! I will never forget those days at the 'HMS Royal Arthur'.

So we ventured back to Hull to school, to continue with our studies for our mate's licence. For me, it was a gruelling time. I was of the opinion that having my bosun ticket would help me along a bit, but now I was wondering if I'd been over-confident. However, towards the end of the course, things started to change.

One day, we were doing chart work. There were two Nigerians taking part in the course, it was the month of February and yes, it was snowing. Well, the looks on the faces of the Nigerian chaps! They asked the teacher (Jim) if they could be moved to another desk and/or room as they were so frightened of the snow! Later on, it stopped snowing, and the winter sunshine appeared. The Nigerian students were OK after that.

The time came to go up to the Board of Trade, which was based in Old Town, so it was within walking distance of the school. We had taken mock exams and had a good build-up to the forthcoming examination. For me, the signals part was no problems, and the same for the orals, but I failed twice on the written exams and it affects you mentally. You start thinking, "Where am I going wrong?" and you have to be careful, as there is a stage where you start to lose faith in what you are doing. I did not want to be there.

Thankfully, things turned out well eventually, and I got my mate's ticket.

The next step was to make an appointment with Hull Fishing Vessels Insurance Company, for them to ask me further questions. I thought this was OK, as we would be sailing with their 'equipment'.

I made my appointment to go up in front of the insurance committee, and there was a retired captain on the board. A lot of questions were asked of me, relating to the River Humber and its buoyage system. I recall that it was something very interesting to me, especially when I had had previously worked on a purpose-built vessel for maintenance of the buoyage system.

Questions were asked on the 'rules of the road' and certain other very important questions.

On completion, the examiner passed me, which I was very pleased about! So, as we were on the fish dock, I immediately walked along to BUT to see what the situation was. Normally, when you have been sailing bosun and acquire your mate's ticket, the company tell you to carry on sailing as bosun for a few trips more, then you are likely to be offered a mate's job.

I arrived at BUT and was chatting to all the people downstairs i.e. ship's runner and ship's husband.

So, when I strolled up, everyone was shaking my hand and congratulating me, and I felt very proud!

The ship's runner/husband approached me and congratulated me. His name was Bob Daubney and he had come in from Ross Group when the companies amalgamated. He asked me what my intentions were and of course I replied, "I would like to sail as mate, as soon as possible." His answer was, "Have you signed the contract?"

Well, we had heard some gossip going around about this certain contract, and if you signed it, you were just giving up on your earnings.

I politely answered Bob by saying, "Sorry Bob; I haven't signed it and I never will." So then Bob must have thought I was being a little sarcastic and he just turned to me and said that I would never get a mate's job with BUT.

I walked away from Bob Daubney thinking "This cannot happen", especially having just spent nearly six months at home for my mate's ticket.

I was passing by Hamling's Office and the runner, Rennie Cawkwell, shouted out to me. I knew Rennie from when I was on the 'St Alcuin' as deckie learner a few years previously, and clearly, he remembered me. He came walking up and asked me what I was doing work-wise, I told him about my mate's ticket etc. and he was pleased for me.

I also told him about the incident with Bob Daubney. Rennie said, "No problem" and offered to sign me on as bosun on the St Loman', which was one of the biggest side trawlers outside of Hull. This was a very good offer, made even better when Rennie added that I could relieve the present mate when he went on his holidays.

So, I signed on the 'St Loman' and was feeling very good about myself.

I got home and explained to my wife what had happened; that I had left the company BUT because I was threatened etc. but would be sailing in a few days on a good ship with another company.

I hadn't got the whole story out of my mouth when there was a loud knock on the door. When I opened it, I saw Jim McPharlane, the company's taxi driver, who had picked me up a few times before, when I had been sailing as spare hand and bosun. I said, "Hello Jim, how's things?" then he spat it out; George Hartley (manager of BUT) was going ballistic as he had found out that I'd signed on the 'St Loman' as bosun!

Jim said he had been ordered by the office to take me down to Hamlings and for me to sign off the 'St Loman' log book and see George Hartley.

So, off we went in the taxi to Hamling's office. I met with Rennie and tried to explain the situation to him. He said, "Don't worry, Ken. This is how it goes, and if you ever need work in the future, come and see me." So that was a nice gesture.

I signed off the 'St Loman' log and proceeded to the BUT buildings to have my chat with George Hartley.

I was ready to give George Hartley what for if he started insulting me! I knew I would always get work as I had a good name, two hands and was capable of doing anything!

On the way to see George Hartley, I passed Bob Daubney and accused him of causing all this trouble. He just looked at me, bewildered, and didn't utter a word.

Then I came face-to-face with George Hartley. He got a little angry about me signing on with the 'competition'. He said that he had recommended I go to school, so in a way, I was his 'protégé' and he was upset about me leaving. Anyhow, he said he had everything sorted, all was OK and for me to forget about any contract as it had already been cancelled.

So, everything was back to normal.

He then asked me what I thought would happen when I went to Hamlings, so I told him what Rennie Cawkwell had told me! So he said, "You were promised a mate's job in a few trips' time, is that correct, Shakesby?" I said "Yes, Mr Hartley," then after several more questions, he began cooling down. He said the plan was for me to sail as mate with BUT, the day after tomorrow! This was the 4th August 1973.

Well, I thought all my birthdays had come at once; I just couldn't believe it! He told me to go outside and ring my wife, then come back in to talk about the situation.

I went to the nearest public phone and called Jean. She was over the moon! After 15 minutes or so I knocked on George Hartley's door and we sat down and started talking tactics.

'Portia'. (Skippers: Maurice Ward, Dave Wooldridge, Dave Grewar, Harry Smith, Ray Jopling and Tommy Atkin). Photograph during the Cod War. Icelandic gunboat close by.

Mr Hartley told me that the trawler I would be going on was the 'Portia'. What a ship she was! Fairly new, diesel, electric, all accommodation aft and a good sea ship. What more could I want? The question I asked was, "Who is the skipper?" (I knew that

101

Maurice Ward was the regular skipper, but I will tell you more about Maurice Ward later). George Hartley told me that the skipper would be Dave Wooldridge and, here is the bombshell. . . it would be my first trip as mate, and Dave Wooldridge's first trip as skipper !!

Never had I seen or heard of this situation before; mate and skipper brand new at the same time. George Hartley asked me what I thought, and I said, "Why not?" I was a young mate, hopefully on the way up, and David, who was a little bit older, was also on the way up, so it could be a good combination.

No more to be said about that situation; George Hartley told me what he expected of me and how he wanted the fish gleaming on the market.

I boarded the 'Portia'. As you can imagine, I felt I was in a kind of dream! When I was introduced to the skipper, we seemed to hit it off directly.

This was August 1973 and we set sail for the Icelandic fishing grounds.

Although I did not know Dave Wooldridge, the skipper, personally, I knew of his older brother, Eddie, and his father, also named Eddie. They had good track records.

It was the summer season, so we were expecting good or reasonable weather. I had time to think about where I was and how lucky I was. I was very thankful. 'The Portia' was a very good ship and accommodation was also good. The crew had been on the ship for a good while; they were all the crew of Maurice Ward, who was having his summer holiday.

The crew members were experienced and I had sailed with some of them previously, as spare hand. I felt that this crew would be dependable.

So, we arrived at south east Iceland and settled down. As I've said, we expected the weather conditions to be not too bad.

We fished up and down the south east area of Iceland. The crew (deck side and bridge) would work 18 hours on, six hours off. So when the skipper went for a nap, I would be in command. It was a good feeling. At that time, I did not know how to haul and shoot the vessel, so the skipper said he would teach me how to haul the nets. I went on the bridge with him at hauling time and after two or three times, I knew what to do. This meant that the skipper could have a little extra time in his bed. When you are up and about for 18 hours and have broken sleep, it's not good. The skipper never complained, though.

The trip was uneventful and we went home with an average catch. The fish room squad and I did a good job of presenting the fish on the market. When the ship got back to Hull, early the next morning, about 5am, it was the mate's job to be on the fish market, watching the fish getting landed and the catch sold.

So there I was, on the fish market, walking up and down to see how the catch was being landed. The ship would have a team of bobbers (who offloaded the fish) then it would be weighed and put into 10-stone aluminium kits, and the man who 'topped off the kit' i.e. laid the top layer, had to make sure it was straight and shiny. The person who did this would receive a small gratuity in turn for his 'extra work'. The rest would be up to the sellers and of course the buyers.

The fish caught first (the oldest) would come out from the ship first, then as the ship started to empty, so the kits would get numbered, so that all involved would know which fish were which. The foreman bobber was in charge of the landing of our trip, so a lot depended on him. I would just like to say this. . . I believe there have been one or two occasions where a foreman bobber has had an attitude and cost the ship a few thousand pounds of revenue.

I picked up quite a bit of money after this trip (especially with me being bosun before) so I bought my wife a brand-new car and paid cash. I'm not boasting; I was always a realist and knew I could come down faster than I went up, so it was a mad impulse buy, and there were never any repeats.

This was what the fishing industry was all about, and I felt good as I knew I had earned the money I received.

While Dave Wooldridge was the skipper, it was good, and the crew liked him. Also, he showed me a lot, which I was very thankful for. Unfortunately, there are always people who are jealous and full of resentment. It was a shame that other grown men said bad things about Dave which were untrue.

The time came, after two trips, for the regular skipper on our ship to come back and for Dave Wooldridge to move on. I knew that George Hartley was giving Dave his 'own ship', so that was good for Dave.

It was a Friday morning and we were due for sailing. Sailing on a Friday was unheard of, so why the company decided to sail us this particular time, I will never know.

I had been thinking a lot about the regular skipper, Maurice Ward. He had a very good name (also his brother was a skipper for BUT) and Maurice had spent a lot of time in the company's stern trawlers, the likes of 'Cassio' ,'Coriolanus' and 'Othello'. He could commission the stern trawlers but had got married and wanted to be on a conventional trawler so that he could maybe get more time at home.

Like I said, I had been thinking a lot about the new skipper. Some people said he was good and others said he was not too good, but time would tell and I would make my own mind up.

When I stepped on board the 'Portia' and was in my cabin, sorting out my clothes etc., this voice behind me said, "Are you the mate?" I looked around and said "Yes." I stand about 5ft 10 inches and this man came up to my shoulders. He said, "Pleased to meet you. I am Maurice Ward, the skipper."

The first thing that came to my mind was that I had expected a taller man! He never seemed high and mighty, but down to earth, which I liked.

When we went to the bridge, he said that if he had been on the last trip, he would not be sailing now! What he meant was that the time and day of sailing were not good. It was only because he'd had a six-week holiday that he'd agreed to sail. I thought, "I'm going to get along OK with the new skipper!"

So we sailed that Friday and all the crew had been sailing with the skipper for quite a while, if not on the 'Portia' then definitely on the stern trawlers, so all was good. I knew I needed to learn a lot from this skipper, as he was one of the best sailing from Hull.

This would have been September or October 1973.

I do look back and think about the time I spent on the 'Portia'. She could be a temperamental lady, but in bad weather, she was a great sea ship to be on.

My trips on board the 'Portia' were good. I had very high regard/respect for the skipper and, as time went by, he was very willing to teach me.

The 'Portia' was built in 1956 and she was the first diesel electric trawler to be built in Hull. Because of this, she was a 'delicate ship'. We would get back to the port and all would be ok, then suddenly we would find electrical problems and have to spend extra time in the dock, which suited me down to the ground, as I had more time to spend with my wife and children.

It was December 1973 and we would be sailing over Christmas, but that was the job. Yes, I really liked staying at home over Christmas, but at this time, the job had to come first.

So, we sailed for the White Sea/Norwegian Coast. At least the weather would be a lot better than Iceland! At this time, I was 26 years old. I felt I was still young and had to learn as much as I could from the skipper.

We started fishing at the North Cape bank and it was a nice job. The weather was good, the fishing was steady and the seabed was nice and flat (so there was little chance of doing any damage to our nets).

It was Christmas eve day, at approximately 9am. The sky was pitch black, as if it were 9pm!

The weather had been turning cold. There was no wind of any particular force, but you could see the black frost on top of the sea and around the decks, and the ice glistening in the dark.

We were all well wrapped up in our winter woollies and had all sorts of clothes on, including the 'duck suit', which kept us dry. I was on the deck with the crew and the skipper was on the bridge, of course. The nets came up and it looked like a very good catch! The cod ends were full and the net was laid out like a big sausage!

After we had hauled the excess net in, we would put a 'becket' around the bellies at amidships, and then the skipper would go slow astern on the engines which, in turn, would bring the net alongside the sip, and we could pull the net and fish in a lot more safely and easily.

I was standing forward in the fish pounds with a tomahawk (boat hook), ready to lean over the bulwarks to hook the float line and, in turn, hook the big lift tackle in and bring the fish in.

I was leaning on the side of the ship and felt I was inches away from the pick-up line. I began stretching and stretching, then the next thing I know, I'm falling into the sea! Everyone will agree; when you go underwater in the North Atlantic, not too far from the Russian coastline, and the visibility is zero, you start wondering, "What will happen?"

As I came to the surface, I could hear voices; especially the skipper! I looked around me. Was I frightened? No! Was I concerned? Yes!

So I swam slowly to where all the fish were in the cod ends (we had a good catch, hence it was floating well!) I pulled myself on and just sat there. Yes, I was wet through and cold, but I knew all would be OK, as crew members were pulling the nets in and I was closer to safety with each moment.

The cod ends came close to the ship and the crew passed down the 'gilson wire', which I took hold of. Then they stared to heave me in.

I came over the bulwark and dropped on the deck, like a big fish, I suppose! I've never been so happy to be laying on a trawler's deck!

The Skipper was still shouting. I am sure he would have been hung out of the bridge windows by his feet!

Well, when I got to my feet, the crew members were asking me if I was OK and I said, "Yes." I felt a bit cold, but that was to be expected!

I was going to carry on with my job, getting the nets in, and as I started moving them, the water inside my protective suit seemed like it was going right down into my boots. The skipper then shouted for me to go inside and leave the bosun to finish off.

I trundled off, walking like a penguin, and by the time I got aft, I was walking more like Frankenstein's monster, my feet felt that heavy!

I took off my wet outer gear (I was bone dry underneath!) then went to my cabin, got a hot bath and a change of clothes and felt much better.

I still feel that the good Lord was looking down on me that day.

After I'd got changed etc. I was summoned to the bridge. The skipper threw all sorts of questions at me; walking around me like a fox with his prey.

I could see that he was so relieved that all was OK with me and I assured him that this would never ever happen again!

We had a steaming mug of tea and I got back on the deck with the crew and carried on working! The crew members were also very relieved I was ok!

That incident happened all those years ago, but I can remember it as if it were yesterday.

That was enough excitement for one trip!

We got home just after the new year and made a nice earner! We were making good money and I was learning (hopefully) all the things I needed.

When Dave Wooldridge was the skipper, he taught me how to haul the nets in. When Maurice Ward came back, he would wake up every three hours to shoot the nets away as I would haul them in. I felt uncomfortable about this situation and he told me not to worry.

Eventually, he taught me to shoot the nets and, as the story goes, it's easy once you know how! I was in my element. All I had to do now was catch as many fish as the others (more, if possible) and do a good job.

I was enjoying my time on the 'Portia' with skipper Ward.

It was the month of April 1974, and skipper Ward was having a couple of trips off. The relieving skipper was called Harry Smith,

I had heard a lot about him. He was a good skipper and senior to the others. The nickname given to him was 'Bumblefoot'!

Skipper Smith was good at his job. On his first trip, he took us down to the east side of Iceland to a place called Langanes, working off a place called Grims Isle. Many years ago, this was a leper colony (hence the name grim?)

We fished the grounds at Iceland and we did well. I recall the fog. . . the visibility was so poor, we could not even see the bow of the ship! It was so tough on our eyes, but we got through it, got home and made a good trip.

The skipper, Harry, asked me if, after I finished on the fish market, I could drop by his house and take him some fish. I said I could, as it was on my way home, anyway. I met the skipper's wife and she was a nice lady. I remember, one time, Harry said something to his wife and she said, "Harry, you may be skipper of your ship, but I am the skipper in this house!" Harry bit his tongue and I was chuckling to myself all the way home!

On the next trip, we sailed to the Norwegian Coast, and it was a good place to fish, as you could only tow one way (northwards) then, when you got to the end of your tow, you would secure your nets and gear, then steam all the way back to the 'starting gate'. Normally you would steam through the night to get to your starting position for first daylight, then repeat the tow.

The depths of water would vary. We would either go shoal or deep, depending on the reports from the other vessels.

I know we had a good trip on the coast. I remember one night, it was blowing about force 7 or 8, and we had caught a lot of fish, but the tackle for heaving the bag of fish forward had come out of the top block and needed to be reinserted.

Yes, yours truly had to go up the mast and rethread the wire back through the block! It was difficult and dangerous, but I had to do it.

At the end of the trip, we had caught about 2,800 kits of fish and a good catch of haddock was included. So, we went steaming home for the market, hoping we would get a good price, which we did.

We enjoyed our time at home, then we had to get ready to sail again. This was April 1974, and we sailed on the afternoon tide. We had been delayed at St Andrews Fish Dock, as we had an electrical problem. We were told all was OK and had just got clear of the dock gates when the chief engineer informed the skipper (Harry Smith) that the problem was still there. We could not go back into the fish dock as the tide was ebbing, so we proceeded to a place across the River Humber called Killingholme, where we would anchor.

We dropped the anchor and the engine room crew worked on the problem, but to no avail. So our instructions were to return to the fish dock on the next high tide, which was the following morning.

With the next tide starting to rise, we picked up our anchor at Killingholme and proceeded back to the fish dock.

Visibility was practically zero and it was cold. Everyone was on standby, preparing the mooring ropes for going back into the fish dock. I was on the bridge, assisting the skipper; along with the poor visibility, the third hand was at the wheel (manual steering when in close quarters to or entering/departing rivers and ports).

The skipper was feeling uneasy with the third hand and I cannot say why, as I knew the third hand and he was a good bloke. Anyhow, the skipper told him to go and sit down in the mess room and we got one of the spare hands to the wheel. I wondered if there had just been a personality clash. Anyhow, there we were, on the bridge, looking at the radar for any other vessels in our area, as well as the channel buoys.

We were closing in on St Andrews Dock, so were swinging the ship round to place the bow into the current/tide for easier, safer control of the ship. At this time, we must have been about one hundred yards or so from the dock. We could hear the fog siren but could see nothing at all.

I looked on our deck and I saw the third hand sitting on the rail, so I shouted "Hey! Come on; get away from there!" And he said, "Aye OK."

The next thing I said was, "Man overboard!" Now, I didn't see anything, it was just something I sensed. Straight away, we called the River Humber Authority and Humber Pilots and all vessels in the area. At that time, the tide was still flooding and it was running strong.

Our crew threw lifejackets and rings into the water to give the man a chance to grab hold of something.

After about 20 minutes, the authorities further down the River Humber said that they had picked up our lifejackets and rings(they had our ship's name on them) but there were no sign of a person.

We took the 'Portia' back into the dock and tied her up just outside BUT. I got a radio call to say "Wait back" as the docks police were going to come down to investigate the missing man.

The police arrived about 30 minutes later and interviewed me regarding what I had seen or heard. I told them everything I could think of. I was quite shaken up.

When the police were satisfied with the statement I gave, they let me go home and said that if they heard anything, they would let me know.

I went down to the dock the following day and found out that the ship had had an electrical fault and that they expected us to stay in dock for about six weeks. That was music to my ears! George Hartley suggested I have a holiday, as this was the first chance I'd had since being mate on the 'Portia'. My wife and I took our children away and we just relaxed and had a good time together.

It was about six weeks later, in the morning, as I was preparing my gear to go back to sea, that there was a knock on the door. I opened it and a police man stood there! He said he would like me to go with him to Hull Mortuary to identify the body they thought could be our third hand! I was absolutely gobsmacked and I was thinking about what someone who had been in the water for all that time would look like.

I said to the policeman, "Why me? Why can't a member of his family go?" The police said they didn't want any mistakes.

The third hand had been a thinnish, gangly chap with pale colouring. I did hear that he had previously had an accident and suffered a head injury, but I was not sure.

The body I saw was large and bloated, with dark skin. I was shocked.

These things happen when someone has been in the water for so long. I felt really sorry for him and his family.

In his pocket he had a small plastic wallet, and inside were his documents. They looked brand new; not wet, damaged or anything!

So the identification was made official and the police thanked me. My wife was waiting for me outside, as she had followed us up to the mortuary. (Jean had not passed her driving test and here she was, following a police car through the town!)

Our third hand had quite a few brothers who also went to sea. I had sailed with a few of them. I knew all his family, and it was a big family. They were good people and they understood what had happened. Mostly, I thought about the man's children.

Then, as a little more time went on, I had to attend the inquest for the crewman. (I do not want to mention him by name, as it will bring back painful memories). Myself and his older brother went to the inquest and it was reasonable. We both spoke about the unfortunate accident, shook hands, bade each other farewell and left.

Fortunately for me, I did return to the 'Portia', along with Maurice Ward (the original skipper). It was good for me to be back, as I was very familiar with the ship and crew.

I stayed on the 'Portia' just about all the time I was mate, except for two trips, which I did on the 'Lord Alexander'. (That story will come later on).

It was time for Maurice to have his two trips off as holiday. He was replaced by a skipper called Tommy Atkin. He came in from Ross Group. The Icelandic Cod War had flared up again and their gunboats were beginning to get really aggressive. It was ironic, I believe, that the Icelandic cutting equipment (which I must admit, was very successful) was originally designed by the British for use during the war, for cutting mines adrift etc.

Me on board 'Portia', during the Cod War. This photograph
was taken on the British frigate was shielding us from the
Icelandic gunboat, which would attempt to cut our warps.

Anyhow, we were down on the east coast of Iceland, fishing off a place called Langanes. The weather was fine and clear, the sea was calm. There were three trawlers towing along and, at a certain position, the three of us would converge on each other, come close, then continue on our intended routes. I cannot remember the name of the third trawler, but the second was one of my old ships, the 'Kingston Emerald', with Brian Boyce as skipper.

The Icelandic gunboat 'Thor'.

His mate was called George Allan, and George was on watch. It was about 3am. Everything had been going fine. Then, on our radar, I picked up a target about nine miles away, coming towards us at slow speed. I mentioned this to George on the VHF, and he said, "Don't worry. It will be someone towing down towards us," but I couldn't accept that.

So what I did, with as little manoeuvring as possible, was to haul our vessel, then we got all the gear inboard and I pretended to shoot our gear away again, so if anyone was looking on their radar, it would seem that we were back in towing mode. It was at this time that the skipper came onto the bridge to see what was happening. Our skipper's name was Tommy Atkin. I told the skipper about the unidentified target and he agreed with my decision.

**One of the British frigates chasing off the
Icelandic gunboat during the Cod War.**

At this point, the vessels converged again and the 'unidentified target' was close to us. The 'Kingston Emerald' was beginning to haul in their nets.

Well, what a turn-up! The unidentified target was, in fact, the Icelandic gunboat 'Thor'! She opened up her searchlights, applied full speed and launched her cutting gear, 'paravane', making a beeline for the 'Kingston Emerald'!

The captain of the Icelandic gunboat was shouting on the VHF that we were fishing illegally etc. and the mate on the 'Kingston Emerald' was absolutely terrified.

I was in command on our bridge and, like I said previously, the 'Portia' was a well-designed vessel, so I proceeded at full speed and got in between the 'Kingston Emerald' and the Icelandic gunboat.

'Arctic Corsair' in collision with an Icelandic gunboat.

115

The Icelandic captain was shouting obscenities at me and told me I was disregarding the laws of the sea, but this was not normal, and he was intent on doing harm to the other ship. I completely ignored him and stayed there, hoping that the 'Kingston Emerald' would get their gear up in time.

We were in very close quarters and the Icelandic captain was still shouting bad words at me over the VHF. The gunboat had to go full astern on the engines so as to prevent a collision, which allowed time for the crew on the 'Kingston Emerald' to get their gear on board, all OK and intact. The skipper on the 'Kingston Emerald' was not very pleased, as he had been woken up. He came to the bridge in a very bad mood, not realising the situation.

Our skipper spoke to him and told him all the events, and the skipper calmed down and was humbled, so all was well.

The Icelandic gunboat went steaming away, with the captain in a very bad mood.

It was not long after that incident that we left for home, with a very poor catch of about 650 kits.

It was a shame, what was happening to our fishing fleet, as it looked like it was coming to an end and was going to be lost through politics. It is ironic, as I believe that Queen

British support vessels encouraging Icelandic gun boats to stop harassing the UK Trawlers.

Victoria was offered Iceland and she refused. If only she'd had the appropriate insight. . . maybe this situation would never have arisen.

Well, we got back to the port and it was decided that the skipper be replaced with another. His name was Dave Grewar and I had sailed with him previously, on the 'Kingston Emerald'. Then I was spare hand and now I was mate, so things would be different, I was sure.

We sailed to south east Iceland to join the main group, who were getting hassled by the Icelandic gunboat. The weather was good (which is always an advantage) and we started fishing.

One of the British frigates protecting UK trawlers
from the Icelandic gunboats.

After a few hours, the gunboat would start its 'operations'. The
trawlers would be riding shotgun, and we had supply vessels and
British naval vessels assisting us. It was really not a good situation
to be in. We were fishing off a place called Langanes and we kept
getting phone calls from the British press to see if we would give
them an interview. Quite rightly, our skipper refused.

The Cod War was beginning to get very dangerous. The Icelandic
gunboat was doing a good job of stopping us fishing! When we
were idle in the water, we could pick up the fish marks below us,
and there were plenty. Also, there were times when the Mother
Ship (carrying the government representative) would call and tell
us to stop fishing, as the government in London were in discussion
with their Icelandic counterpart. It was horrendous.

Our skipper decided to shoot the trawl and, no sooner as the trawl
was on the bottom, the gunboat was on us. Our skipper called up
the 'British Destroyer' and they were alongside us within minutes.
The skills of the person manoeuvring the British vessel were
absolutely first-class; it stayed so close to us that the Icelandic
gunboat could not get near.

We got our trawl back inboard and our skipper, to say the least,
was not in a good mood. He was blaspheming over the VHF!

118

Anyhow, when all was secure on deck, I went to the bridge and the skipper was looking worse for wear. He decided to go to his cabin.

Before he went, the skipper gave me my orders, which were to steam to a bank called Hari Kari and have a tow there, to see if there was anything there. If not, I was to return to the main group of trawlers.

I followed my orders. (We were a good distance from the main group, so there was no hassle from the Icelandic gunboat). Unfortunately, the fishing prospect was not good, so we returned. We could only shoot our nets away every so often, when the Icelandic gunboat had gone somewhere else.

The situation was soul-destroying for everyone. We managed to scrape a trip together of about 1000–1100 kits of fish. Meanwhile, the Icelandics were pushing us to a limit of 200 miles from their shoreline, which would have made it impossible for the trawling industry to operate from the UK.

Maurice Ward had been on holiday and was still resting at home. I do believe he was not too interested in coming back to a ship which was going to Iceland, as the stress was too much and the financial gain not enough. (He passed away in early 2009. I owe that man lots for helping me, and I will always respect and remember him).

During my time as mate on the 'Portia', I sailed with a lot of good people and I would like to think that I helped them in their careers.

There was a man I knew very well (or I thought I did) and he had a bosun's ticket, so I signed him on with us as third hand, (one position below bosun) to relieve the regular man. Anyhow, he was good at the job and will appear further down the line.

Christmas was coming up. I had been checking my sea time to see how many days I needed to do before I could go back to school for my skipper's certificate. I was very surprised and disappointed to find that I was short by 19 days. I was so down; I thought I would never get my chance.

'Lord Alexander'. (Skipper Maurice Ward).

Then out of the blue came my saviour!

I had a telephone call from Maurice Ward, and he asked me if I would be interested in going mate with him on the 'Lord Alexander'. Of course, I jumped at the chance, knowing that I would get my sea time in, which would enable me to go to school.

I signed on the 'Lord Alexander' and she was an old girl, but strong and sturdy; a very good sea ship!

We sailed on the 1st December 1974 and I was enrolled to start college for my skipper's ticket the following January. I thought, "This is great! What more could I ask for; to do this trip to the White Sea and be home before Christmas, then start studying for my skipper's ticket!"

We sailed to the White Sea and the weather was very good; no bad storms or anything. We caught a very good catch, really; no one could ask for anything more!

When we got home, I went on to the market, and the catch was all laid out, looking very good. The only problem was that there were no buyers, with it being Christmas. The usual buyers had clearly decided to celebrate by getting drunk! Consequently, no one turned up to buy the catch. I was fuming, as the catch looked really fresh.

Later in the day, I went down to the office to settle up and ended up having to pay back 200 pounds as our overheads had been greater than the money we got from the catch! I was so disappointed.

On the positive side, I had achieved the sea time I needed for my skipper's. So, I arranged to get my 'heavy gear' from the 'Lord Alexander' (consisting of my work clothes, sea boots etc) as I knew I wouldn't be needing it for quite a number of months.

I started at Hull College in January 1975. With a lot of the content from my mate's ticket still fresh in my mind and having spent a good spell onshore with my wife and children, I felt ready for the course and ended up really enjoying it.

From the authorities, I was getting paid 14 pounds per week, which was not much. Then again, it was better than nothing, and we managed to get by.

In the July, I sat my examination, and my oral examination was given to me by Captain Disden; the same captain who took me for my mate's ticket. I felt good, especially when Captain Disden said to me, "That's fine, Mr Shakesby. You have passed." It was like a big weight had been taken from my shoulders. I was really feeling good.

I ran home (we had a car but, as of now, I couldn't drive, ha ha) and when I told my wife, good times were had by all!

I rested at home for a few days, just letting the reality sink in about my ticket, and then I went down to the dock to see Mr George Hartley. We had a good conversation and he told me what to expect from the future.

When I came downstairs from Mr Hartley's office, there were a lot of skippers and mates standing outside, chatting away. They all congratulated me and asked me if I was getting signed on, to which I answered, "I don't know."

Chapter 8
IN COMMAND

One or two days later, I decided to have a walk down to the dock to see if anything was happening, as I wanted to get back to work to earn some more money. Six months onshore is a long time!

When I got to the dock, I was chatting with the other lads when the ship's husband came outside and said, "Ken, George Hartley wants to see you." I was a bit surprised at this. I thought it would probably be an informal chat, and that he might arrange for me to go mate on one of the vessels. That was the normal thing, when you got your skipper's ticket; the company would ask you to sail as mate for a few trips, then if they thought you had potential, they would promote you to skipper.

I knocked on George Hartley's door and he called, "Come in."

We chatted about the industry and he told me that there were a few 'top money-earning skippers' waiting to be signed on. I agreed with him. He said, "Look out the window and see all the skippers waiting for work". I thought I would be back of the queue.

'Ross Otranto', (skipper Ken Shakesby).

Then, all of a sudden, he puts it to me. He said, "OK, skipper Shakesby; I have decided to give you your skipper's start. You will be sailing the day after tomorrow on board the 'Ross Otranto.'"

I did not know what to say! I was dumbfounded. Not only was I getting my first ship as skipper, but the 'Ross Otranto' was the second biggest conventional trawler in the UK!

This was amazing for me.

He said, "What do you think to that?" and I was over the moon! He said I would be relieving the regular skipper for two trips (the normal system), then if all went well, he would put me on a ship of my own! At that moment, I was thinking, "Not bad for someone who is twenty-eight years old!"

Everyone, my wife, family and friends, were over the moon for me, and my dad was especially pleased for me.

The 'Ross Otranto' had been in a shipyard in South Shields, so I had to go there to sail the vessel.

When I got on board, the crew I knew me, as I had sailed with them all throughout my fishing days, so at least I knew what type of crew I had with me and yes, they were a good crew to be with.

We sailed, and our destination was south east Iceland, around the Whaleback area. The fishing was not abundant, but I thought, what with the other ships' reports being not too good, it would be best to be patient and keep a steady average catch for each haul. I did that and never went steaming about, so the 'gear' was mostly on the bottom.

When our time was up, we left for home. Although I didn't break any records, I was up there with the 'top skippers', so I did not feel too disappointed with myself. The crew got a good pay-off too, so all was well, and I had one more trip before the regular skipper came back.

We landed back at Hull and I had a few days at home, then sailed again on my second trip on board the 'Ross Otranto', back to Iceland. I'd been expecting the owners to tell me to sail for the White Sea/Norwegian Coast, but I was not destined to have a trip there, as it seemed I was deemed an Iceland man!

Again, we shot away the nets at south east Iceland, around the Whaleback and Bullnose area. This time, it looked bleak. Steady reports were coming in from further north, so we lashed the gear in and went steaming up to the Isafjord area. Again, the fishing was steady. The worst thing, psychologically, would be steaming about and chasing the fish, so I just towed up and around the east side of Iceland, around Grims Isle and Langanes.

We sailed back to Hull with a 'middle of the road' catch. It was on par with other vessels in the area, but I still felt it could have been better.

When we landed, the manager was happy with the financial side of things but told me that the regular skipper would be coming back, as he had been on the ship for a few years. He said he would put me back as mate.

My ego was slightly damaged, but I looked at the bigger picture; I would have my time, and I had youth on my side.

I signed on the 'Loch Eriboll' for two trips as mate, with Dave Paterson as skipper.

'Loch Eriboll'. (Skipper Dave Paterson).

I then signed on the 'Portia' as mate; it seemed she would be my destiny! To be fair, it was like coming home! A lot of the regular crew members were there, and we had a good reunion.

This time, we were sailing for Iceland and, politically, it was not too good, as the Icelandic Government was really clamping down on restrictions for foreign trawlers; especially the British trawlers. Things were getting worse.

The Icelandic Government was pressing to stretch their fishing limits out to 200 miles, which would be a catastrophe for the British Fishing Industry. We were reassured by our government that they were doing everything possible to get a reasonable quota situation with the Icelandics.

So, our instructions was, "Business as usual."

So, we set sail for the east side of Iceland. Our fleet were mainly in that area and the plan was to keep together; strength in numbers.

We arrived, and the picture was not too good. The trawlers were scattered about, which meant there was not much fish, as all the vessels were searching.

Just to give you an idea, on an 18-day trip to Iceland, ships were expected, on average, to bring home at least 1,000 kits. Depending on market prices, 1,000 kits would be financially reasonable.

We had the Royal Navy on the scene, along with tugs and supply vessels, (these were contracted to the Ministry of Defence). It was thought that support vessels would make things more secure, but in reality, there was not a lot of fish around, so the trawlers had to spread out anyway.

This was good for the Icelandic gunboat, as it could sneak up during dark hours or in poor visibility, strike at a trawler and cut its warps. It would take the trawler a good while to install another trawl and be prepared for fishing again, and the revenue would be lost. As I said previously, it was soul-destroying.

We fished up and down the east side of Iceland and I can't remember a bleaker time. I suppose, when I think back, the way the skippers looked at things was that we had to be (one) fishing in a group and (two) plodding up and down. No one could ask for anything else. For me, this was unacceptable, as the crews still had to earn money to take home to their families. It was just not a good situation to be in, and the future looked even more grim.

It was August 1976; summer time. Normally, all the regular skippers take their annual holidays in the summer months, as that is when the fishing becomes slack; allowing 'newcomers' a chance.

George Hartley informed me that I would be signing on the 'Kingston Beryl' as skipper, which was very good news! The 'Kingston Beryl' was not too bad a ship, but for some reason, she never seemed to catch as much fish as the other ships!

So here I was again, with another vessel under my command.

I had a brief chat with George Hartley before we sailed for Iceland.

We stopped at south east Iceland, close to the group, and shot the trawl. I showed patience and it paid off. The mate with me was a chap called Wally Atkinson, and we were at college together for our skipper's ticket. I remember that a couple of years previously, I had been third hand on board the 'Kingston Amber' and Wally had been mate. Talk about cat and dog; we were always arguing! Don't get me wrong; Wally was a first-class mate and I had the utmost respect for him, it's just that we had different views. I was just hoping that he would not hold it against me that I was skipper while he was still mate!

'Kingston Beryl'. (Skipper Ken Shakesby).

Once we got clear of the river and any would-be obstacles, me and Wally sat down and had a good chat, True to form, Wally was a great chap. We talked and laughed about our time together on the 'Kingston Amber' and I believe we formed a bond. He was a great chap to have on your side.

Anyhow, like I said, we shot away on the south east side and did a trip of about 20 days, which was not too bad, as the longer we are away, the more the vessel's running expenses increase, so in reality it was good to do a reasonably quick trip (around 20 days) and for everyone to get a decent settling (pay-off) from it.

The 'Kingston Beryl' was doing ok. Yes, sometimes we had our problems i.e. engine room breakdowns and bad weather stoppages, but this was part and parcel of the job.

I recall that we were fishing around the south east Iceland area; places call Kidney Bank, Bullnose, and Whaleback. The fishing was quiet and all the 'big guns' were happy enough, staying in a group just plodding away.

Just a few miles away was a bank called Hari Kari and there were lots of wrecks around, so when you were towing your gear, you had to be very careful, as you could lose it on one of the wrecks. (These were vessels from World War II). Anyhow, we had our sister ship with us, and the skipper was called Barry Turner; originally from Ross Group. He asked me if I fancied going with him to search at Hari Kari Bank, so I said "Yes, OK."

All the other ships came up on the 'box' (VHF radio) and said "We have already been there and there is nothing! As bare as a badger's bottom!"

So Barry and I steamed to Hari Kari. It was only about 20-25 miles away and we were just on the edge of the VHF radio range, which meant that if me and Barry spoke to each other and had something good to report, all the other ships would hear the message, then they would come charging across and what little fish we had found would be scooped up in a jiffy! So we decided to go onto 'low power'. Ships which were close would pick our conversation up.

When we arrived on the bank, we decided to split up; one of us go on one side of the bank and the other on the other. So we shot the gear out and we were towing about 22-25 lengths of warp (towing wire) which is deep, as it takes longer to haul and shoot the gear.

We shot away and did one tow; nothing much to report, but it did look promising, as the fish that dropped on the deck were strong and lively.

We caught about 40 baskets in a three-hour tow, which wasn't too bad. It was better than what they were catching at Kidney Bank!

We had a company schedule which meant we had to report our position and catching rate to the company. We reported similar rates to the ships at the Kidney area, just in case anyone decided to come and have a look at us!

We were towing along to get closer to the 'Kingston Pearl' (Barry) and when we were pretty close, he came across on the VHF and said, "Get close to me and haul your gear," which I did, and when we hauled it, the net came to the surface like a submarine! It was a great sight to see. All the crew on deck were cheering. I could see that the cod ends were pretty full of cod, haddock, coley and swaddies (a deep-water redfish).

In those days we had a Decca Navigator System (even then it was antiquated) but nothing else. Linked up to the navigator was a plotter and yes, it plotted your course. When all conditions were good, i.e. clear signals to the navigator, then it was good.

So back to the start. . . while we were working Hari Kari Bank, I decided to use the plotter, and when this good haul popped up, I just went back over the tow and made a few minor changes, and we came up with a bigger catch! Yes the trawl did get torn a bit (it was to be expected in places like Hari Kari Bank) so while the crew brought the fish in, I would jump from the bridge (wheel house), taking a couple of the crew with me, and start repairing the trawl, so that when all was finished with the decking of the fish, we would only be a couple of minutes more, then the trawl was ready to go.

For me and the crew, this fishing was our saviour, and I was also trying to keep it quiet from the other ships, so we had to be careful what we reported and what we said on the box. Conversation was kept to a minimum.

We were towing all about Hari Kari Bank still using the plotter. I would put down any obstructions i.e. wrecks, dangerous ground etc. We really boosted our trip with this fish; especially at the end of the trip, as it would be really fresh for the market.

The 'Kingston Pearl' was the first to leave the area and start steaming home, and when the skipper, Barry Turner, reported to the company what he had on board, you can imagine what our other company ships was saying! I cannot print what the conversation consisted of, but believe me, there were a lot of strong words involved!

So as it happened, all the other ships from around came steaming up to me, demanding to know what was going on, and the answer was simple; they were all afraid to leave the main group in case someone caught a few more baskets of fish than the other! For me, it was pathetic.

First and foremost, my job was to take care of my ship and crew's welfare, and that is what I did. I just kept towing up and down around the bank and around wrecks, and I was content. The fish came on board steadily and in good supply. Then the office decided to call me home, so we lashed everything up and set sail.

We landed and made a good price. The manager was very pleased with the outcome, and so was I. Everyone on board had worked hard and deserved to get a good pay-off, which they did.

I can vaguely remember another trip back to Iceland on the 'Kingston Beryl' and again we stopped at the south east side of Iceland. The weather was not good and eventually we managed to scrape a trip of 1000 kits. When I sent the information to the office, they told me to return home. So off I went again. We did a trip of 18 days, and the settling was good; especially for me, as it was a quick trip, so the expenses were not too high.

Some of the skippers were like children, they were so immature. I remember a chap called Brian Owbridge, who, because I had done better than him at Iceland, would not talk to me! There were a few immature skippers around still.

The next trip was a testing one for me. We were into December 1976, sailing just before Christmas, to the Norwegian Coast/ Barents Sea areas. To me, it seemed like going to a different world! There would be no gunboats to worry about, and when you went to have some sleep, you could feel relaxed, rather than sleeping with one eye open! It was so good.

We arrived and got in with the other ships, but unfortunately the weather conditions were very bad. We kept up as best we could, but for a good amount of the trip, we were 'laid and dodging'. The weather was horrendous.

We hung in there and eventually came to the end of our trip. I will just tell you what happened. The mate on board with me at the time was the husband of my wife's sister and he was a friend. At least, that's what I thought, as not only did I get him a job as third hand, I managed to get him on the 'Kingston Beryl' with me, as mate. But unfortunately, people have short memories, as today, the same man is someone who thinks he is better than the rest and tends to forget about the people who helped him. Really, this situation makes me angry, as I helped a few people and now they don't give me the time of day!

Anyhow the 'sparks' (radio operator) approached me and said, "Skipper, there is a telegram at Wick Radio for us and I just cannot get it." I told him not to worry as maybe the conditions etc. were stopping us from receiving the telegram. At that time, everything was done by Morse key, so I did not feel uncomfortable about it.

When eventually we got the telegram, the radio operator said, "Skipper, please sit down as this is bad news." I looked at him strangely, then read the telegram and nearly fell over. I had a brother-in-law called Melv, who was initially my friend, then married my sister and we all used to pal about together. So not only was he my brother-in-law, he was my best friend. The telegram was from the owners and it stated, "We regret to inform you that your brother-in-law, Melvyn Stephenson, has been killed in a tragic boating accident."

I just felt faint. We were at the Norwegian Coast, towing along. Fishing was slack and the weather bad, so it was not good at all,

I called to the mate on deck and he came up to the bridge. I showed him the telegram; he also knew Melv (the fishing industry was a tight community). I told the mate to watch the ship while I went to my cabin.

I stayed in my cabin alone and had a cry. It was not right that my friend and brother-in-law, at the age of 28 years, should be robbed of his life. I was absolutely gutted. I thought of my sister, who had four small children, and Melv's family and friends. It was hard to take it all in.

I sat there, thinking of all these things, and as the trip had been a hard one, on the spur of the moment, I told the mate, "Get the gear in and secure it; we are off home."

The first thing I did was call my sister. I knew my wife would be with her, helping out. I spoke to my sister and, of course, she was in a terrible state. I then spoke to my wife, and she told me the day of the funeral. I knew, with the current weather conditions, we wouldn't make it home in time.

The chief engineer, Pete Willey, whom I had known for a long time, since I was a small child, found out what was going on and said, "Don't worry, skipper, we will get you home."

We started steaming for home and I knew it was just about impossible to get to the dock before the funeral service began. We were hitting gales of forces 8-9; it was horrific. The crew members never uttered a word about how bad the weather was, or how things were getting thrown across the galley and mess room. The weather was unbelievable.

I think back to those dark days and I do believe the good Lord was watching over me, the ship and the crew.

We arrived at the River Humber; I had been in constant touch with my family and my company, so they were aware of the situation.

We got alongside Albert Dock in Hull, the morning of Melv's funeral. At the dockside, my wife was waiting in the car, ready to get me home to bathe and change etc. Also on the dock was the company ship's husband, who had authority to take the ship through the lock pits and secure the vessel at the dockside, ready for offloading the catch the next morning. This saved me a lot of time.

My wife drove us home, and you can imagine the things we wanted to talk about, but we just could not get the words out.

I managed to get bathed and changed and went to see my sister and Melv's family, prior to the service. It was terribly sad.

There were people lining the streets, from Melv's mother's home, to the church. It was just unbelievable.

We attended the funeral and the service was nice; consisting of all Melv's family and friends. I knew that wherever Melv was, he was looking over us and smiling.

Melv was put to rest, and maybe later in the book I will tell you about the enquiry into Melv's accident.

I was soon to be heading off to sea again, and I got a call from my manager to go and have a talk with him. I got to his office and we chatted about things in general, and then he got down to business. We started talking about his intentions and where he would send me for my next voyage. What he told me I could not believe; he was going to send me to home waters, which was around the Shetland Isles and the north side of the Orkney Isles and/or Faroe Island. I thought this was ridiculous.

The reason for this, George said, was that the company's quotas were just about done for the year, so his hands were tied. His options, for me, were the north side of Scotland (home waters) or East Greenland. East Greenland was out, for me, as I had heard that all the stern fishers were being pushed out of there, due to the ice and bad weather, so there was no chance of me, on the 'Kingston Beryl', going there. I pointed this out to the manager and he just gave me a look.

I happened to see the company morning schedule; one of our vessels, the 'Loch Eriboll', was working Iceland. I said to the manager, "Let me go to the same place as the 'Eriboll'" and he got very angry with me and said it was impossible. I felt that something underhanded was going on; maybe the skipper of the 'Loch Eriboll' was a 'blue-eyed boy' and shouldn't be there, but people would keep quiet, providing he was catching fish.

So, no more to be said, I was destined for the home water deal.

We sailed a couple of days later and I was not feeling very good about it, as I could not for the life of me see any profit in the outcome.

We arrived on the north coast of Scotland and shot the gear. The weather was not too good. We towed along for a few hours and hauled the net. I remember thinking there would probably be more fish in our local wet fish shop than there were in the trawl; it was pathetic! So, after a few tows, we hauled the gear in, lashed it down and went steaming towards Faroe Island.

Faroe, to a trawlerman, has always been OK, for when you are steaming home and you have a few hours to kill, you shoot the nets and may catch a few baskets of fish; although certainly nothing to get excited about. Sometimes you would hear that someone had come up with a decent catch, but this happened very rarely. You certainly did not want to start your trip coming here! It was demoralising, to say the least, and continued like this for a while.

We would shoot the gear away, have a couple of tows, then bring in the gear and secure it, before steaming back to around Foula (north of Orkneys) and repeat. It was getting too much for me.

Not only was this crippling me psychologically, but when I looked at the company schedule, all the vessels (or most of them) were sailing to the Norwegian Coast, where you could be 90 per cent sure you would be going home with a decent catch!

This particular haul, at Faroe, we pulled in the nets and, again, had maybe two or three baskets of fish. So I called out to the deck to "drop the doors in". Usually, when that is called, the ship is going for a long steam. So, of course, the crew looked at me as if to say, "There is nowhere we can go."

Well, needless to say, the doors got dropped in and the trawl secured, and I set a course off for the Norwegian Coast to the 'starting gate'. From here we would just tow up to the north, shoot the gear, then haul, then shoot, and continue with this system until the end of the day. Then you would heave in the gear and steam back through the night. The water depths ranged; for example, you could follow up to the north on the 100 fathoms line or go as deep as 200 fathoms, or you could just tow on the banks, which let you tow in any direction, as the current was not an issue.

All the ships were around the big freezer trawlers and conventional trawlers. There were quite a few of the big boys around!

During my steaming across from Faroe to the Norwegian Coast, I was sending in our morning position and just inserting 's/s', which means 'still steaming'. Of course, the manager wanted to know what I was doing, but I could not inform him; at least not until I had reached the Norwegian Coast. I appreciate that he was very angry with me and I had a feeling this trip was going to be my last as skipper with BUT.

Nevertheless, I was intent on catching a trip, so at least the crew would get some financial gain for the torment they had been through.

So, we got to the starting gate, shot away the trawl and starting towing towards the north. We did this for several tows and changing water depths, to see if I could improve the catch. We did OK; nothing outstanding. It was certainly a lot better than at Faroe! Then I decided to shoot on the bank and, talking to the other skippers, found out there had been a shoal of coley come through. Some of the ships got lucky and caught some of this.

They told me to be careful as, if we saw this mark on the sounder, it would look similar to a haystack, which seemed to me to be a lot of fish! We shot the trawl and started towing and, at that time, the ships were well scattered, looking for this so-called haystack. So, we had a couple of tows and the catch was good. It started to give me some faith back and I felt good for the crew. I was nice and relaxed on the bridge, just towing along. The weather was good, and we were catching a mixture of cod, coley and haddock, so it was looking OK.

I glanced at the echo sounder as I was sitting in the chair and behold, what did I see on the screen, but a mark which looked like a massive thumbprint which had been dipped in ink! This was it; this was the haystack everyone had been looking for! I called the ships around me, as we needed to keep track of this shoal. I passed over the mark and about 20 minutes later, I hauled in the nets.

The fish were floating in the cod ends well before the doors were up. The sight was fantastic! What an amazing feeling it was for everyone. By the time the doors were up and we were heaving on the nets, the fish had settled down in the trawl and it was full!

It took us quite a while to get the fish on deck and when it was completed, both sides of the fore deck were full of fish! What a sight. We kept the trawl on deck until we could start gutting the fish, then sent it down to the fish room. Once we had made a working space, then we shot the trawl and started towing again. I think the towing time was only about one hour, so it was so good to see this.

We got a few more passes at this fish, then, as quickly as it came, it was gone again. But me and the other crew members were feeling good, as we knew this trip would not be futile after all! I had been without sleep for a long time, so now was the time to get my head down for a few hours, with a little bit of a contented feeling.

The contents of the catch were coley, haddock and cod, so it was money in our pockets.

Each night, we towed onto the bank, which was shoal water, and you could tow anywhere, which was a good thing, as the British fleet was all together, within a radius of three miles.

Then the time came for me to get the trawl inboard and secure it, for we were commencing our run home. I felt reasonably OK, as we had a catch of about 1600 kits of fish, which was considerably more than we would have caught in home waters.

We arrived home safely and the mate informed me the next day that the catch was looking good on the fish market then. I found out we had made a good financial catch. So, overall, I was pleased with the decision I had made a few weeks earlier to leave the home waters and steam across to the Norwegian Coast.

I went to the office the next morning to have a talk about the trip etc. with my manager. I was getting a bit stressed out, as I knew I would be in a little bit of trouble. My manager called me into his office and he seemed OK. Then we discussed the voyage. He was happy with the end result, which had made the company a decent profit. Then, out of the blue, he told me I was fired! When I asked him why, he said he was impressed with the decision I made, but it went against his feelings!

I told him that I knew I was not included in his little circle of friends, so it was difficult for me to achieve better things. This he disagreed with. The discussion was becoming heated, then he repeated that I was fired! I could not accept this and told him, "Sorry, Sir, but you cannot fire me, for the simple reason that I resigned last night, as soon as I secured the vessel to the dockside." He was furious!

So, I received my salary cheque from him and dismissed myself from the office.

At that time, I didn't let it bother me too much. Yes, I was angry with the way I had been treated, but I was not included in the company's 'circle'. I met my wife and briefly told her what had happened.

I was on a learning curve; some good things, some bad. I had to meet another BUT manager upstairs, who was in charge of the stern/freezer trawlers. He asked me my opinion of the stern trawlers and we discussed certain things. He wanted me, eventually, to go as skipper on one. So I said I would try it. The manager decided to sign me on as first mate on the 'Cassio'; a very nice ship, which was new and modern. The skipper of the 'Cassio' was called Tony Atkinson; I had previously worked with him on the 'Kingston Emerald', so we knew each other very well, which was good.

'Cassio'. (Skipper Tony Atkinson).

I joined the ship and expected to be away between eight and 12 weeks (which seemed like a prison sentence, but if these were the ships of the future, I had to go and see). I boarded the vessel and the skipper showed me to the bridge and controls etc. as all the controls to the deck equipment were operated from the bridge and, of course, the propulsion. It was the biggest bridge I had seen, and I had never seen so many control buttons/levers/switches in my life! I was taken aback. I said to the skipper, "I will never get the hang of all these!" and he assured me that I would be able to do it all 'with one hand' within a week!

St Andrews dock lock pits

Looking towards Lordline building

The skipper was right! I know it was a long trip, but for me, it was something new, with modern equipment on board and all new galley equipment. When you came off the deck, you immediately had to take off your boots and put your inside shoes/slippers on! The industry was moving forward; it was good!

The crew were more settled, as they had working watches of 12-hour work and six-hour rest, which really was unheard of, so all the crew benefitted from this new kind of trawler.

Again, on the 'Cassio', we were fishing at Norwegian North Cape and up in the Barents Sea towards the Russian Coast. The job was really good, as there was the skipper and me, plus second and third mates, so it was a good system. My job, really, was to do 12 hours on the bridge and 12 hours off, relieving the skipper, and the more I got into it, the more I liked. Unfortunately, the problem for me was the time away. Sometimes the days would really drag.

This particular day, we were fishing up in the Barents Sea when we got a call from a Russian naval vessel for permission to board. Of course, we agreed. At this time, our gyroscope for automatic steering and true compass system were down, as the liquid in the bowl was infected with bacteria, so of course we could not use our automatic steering. When the Russian officers came to the bridge, they saw our gyro sphere all hung up, and we then told them the story. They told us to carry spare liquid and offered some of theirs, which was so good of them.

I asked the officer who was going back to the naval ship if he could do me a very big favour and give me one of their country's flags, 'hammer and sickle'. He said "No" and was very nervous, so I told him to please forget it, as I did not want to cause any problems.

So, off the Russian crew went back to their ship and in the meantime, our skipper took some rum out of our bonded stores and parcelled it up for the Russian crew. They returned, cleaned out our system, then poured the new liquid in and checked everything.

The skipper then gave them the box of Hull Rum, which was made only for trawlers from the local bonded stores. The Russian crew members were over the moon and we asked them if they needed anything else. We gave them some English food and so on, and they really liked us. Then, one of the officers came up to me and gave me a brand-new flag of Russia ('hammer and sickle')! This was really good for me, as my son collected flags as a hobby, and he would be so pleased about this one! The officer begged me not to use it in public, which I promised. It stayed within my house.

So handshakes were in order, and 'thank you's. The Russian crew went back to their naval vessel and we carried on doing our fishing. We all agreed that the Russian team were excellent people.

In the end, we were away around 12 weeks. Financially, this was not very advantageous, so I wanted to get back onto the 'Portia' for some hard-earned cash!

I explained to Tony, the skipper of the 'Cassio', that the stern trawler/freezers were not for me. I did enjoy working on them, but I would feel more at home on a conventional trawler.

I was asked on numerous occasions to work on the stern trawlers, including a BUT stern trawler going to the Australian Bight, but I was not interested. For me, there was no buzz or challenge to it.

My children would often ask if they could see the ships. One day, I took them onto a vessel, and it was so sad, as the vessel was in darkness. I was feeling about and my daughter, Lisa, fell down some stairs. I went absolutely berserk at the watchman and was so thankful that my daughter was OK, apart from some scrapes to her legs.

There are some things that stay in your mind forever. Being in the fishing industry is certainly one of them.

I stayed at home for a short while and was then given a job as mate on board the 'Lord St Vincent', and we sailed to the White Sea. The fishing was below average, what with bad weather and there being not many fish around.

Chapter 9

AN END AND A BEGINNING

I stayed at home for a few weeks. It was around January 1978, and the fishing industry was declining rapidly. I tried to adjust, to see what the future might hold for me in the deep-sea trawling industry. I could take a chance and maybe do a few trips here and there, then maybe go on the unemployment system for a while. There was a lot to think about; including the welfare of my wife and three children.

The manager called me and said he was putting me on the 'Lord St Vincent' as mate, as at that moment, there were very limited opportunities. I thought I had better take it, as it was a job, at least. Plus, at this time, the fishing areas were all closing down, and trawlers were being 'laid up'.

I signed on the vessel and we sailed to the Barents Sea. It was winter time, of course, but the weather was not too bad. The skipper had very little faith; as if we were going through the motions for nothing.

If I remember rightly, I did maybe two trips more. Financially, it was a disaster. Then I spoke to Tom Neilson, who was the secretary of the Hull Trawler Skippers and Mates Guild and had an office on the fish dock. He told me that many Hull skippers had left the industry to look for better things, and that there was openings in the Gulf of Suez in Egypt.

I thought it over and spoke to my wife. We assessed our options and decided that this would be the way to go, as the fishing industry was dying with each day that passed.

As you can gather, my career as a deep-sea trawlerman was coming to an end. I felt that there were lots of other things waiting for me.

From starting in the fishing industry to this date, I can honestly say that I do not regret it for one moment. I have had both bad times and good times and met some very good people. Fishing is in my blood, and that is how it will be for the rest of my life.

I left the fishing industry with sadness that this part of my life had come to an end.

So, I had spent the first 15 years of my career in freezing working conditions and here I was, about to start in a somewhat hotter climate. Please read on!

I bade loving farewells to my wife and family and went across to Egypt. Bear in mind, I had never been anywhere like this, so the people and culture were all brand new to me! Initially, my thought was that I would go as a mate, to learn the job, then see how things transpired.

I arrived in Cairo and the company I would be working for was called Gulf Fleet Incorporated; an American company owned by Houston Natural Gas. This was around March 1978.

I met the Cairo management and stayed overnight in a hotel, ahead of travelling to the job site the next day. I remember, at that time, the President of Egypt was a man called Anwar El Sadat.

I had never been on oil field supply vessel, so this was brand new to me! The car picked me up around six the following morning and away I went. The driver was, of course, local, so his command of the English language was limited and my knowledge of Arabic was absolutely zero!

As far as I could understand, the journey to the job site would take about five hours, so I just sat back and visualised what might be in store for me.

After about three hours, we stopped at a roadside cafe and had a cup of tea etc.

During the drive, much to my disappointment, all we saw was desert and nothing else!

We finally arrived at the 'base camp', which was situated south of the Gulf of Suez. As this was 1978, there was still some uneasiness between Egypt and Israel.

I slept at the 'base camp' and, the following morning, was driven down to the dock. (When I say 'dock', I mean a place cut out of the desert on the edge of the Gulf of Suez. The jetty was built up of sand and an outer stone wall, which acted as a breaker from the prevailing wind and sea conditions).

A sister ship of 'Gulf Fleet 3'.

This was the first time I had been close to an Anchor Handling Tug Supply oil field supply vessel, and first impressions were good! The vessel I was joining was the 'Gulf Fleet 3'.

I got on board and the master was called Dennis. He was from the London area and previously a lorry driver, which seemed strange to me! He seemed a good chap, but I believe his rank went to his head a little bit.

When I was introduced to him, he had a tan on him like a local resident and just wore shorts and a t-shirt, which I did not think was suitable attire.

So we sailed up north. In the Gulf of Suez, there are traffic separation lanes for vessels and the north-bound one was the lane closest to the Sinai Peninsula, which was still controlled by Israel. So, for instance, if any vessel (sometimes us) wandered out of lane slightly, the Israeli Navy would command them to go back, staying close until they did. The Navy were always around.

We would have drilling equipment on our decks, and below decks, we carried bulks i.e. cement, barite, fuel, water etc. to supply the rig.

We arrived at the rig, secured well and commenced discharging our cargo. For me, it was so interesting, as in my previous job, it was very rare to have close contact with other vessels or units, so I was very interested in the work.

Eventually, I decided, "if you can't beat them, join them!" So I put my shorts and a t-shirt on and was on deck, organising the local crew in their duties.

Once our decks were cleared of cargo, we would become a safety/standby vessel for the rig, in case any emergencies arose. I set the crew up with cleaning the vessel and, if weather conditions permitted, we would do some chipping and painting; general maintenance work, to keep the ship looking good.

The mistake I made was getting so involved with the work that I didn't realise the sun was so strong and, consequently, ended up looking like a tomato! The pain got pretty bad, and I knew it would be worse the next day.

I did what I could to ease the pain; got some cream and kept cooling down my skin. I had a terrible night's sleep and was shaking and sweating from heatstroke. The following morning, I could not keep off the toilet. It was sheer agony.

Needless to say, once back to normal, I vowed I would never ever do that again!

My contract was 90 days on the boat, with 30 days' holiday. I thought this was a good deal, and there was time for improvement and promotion.

This second industry of mine would take me to numerous countries, as you'll read. I was like a child with a new toy, as this was something completely different to what I had been doing.

We were doing three months, which was a long time, and yet I had done that a number of times on the stern freezer fishing vessels.

I was moved around the supply vessels for about 12 months as mate, so that I could get experience in all fields of the offshore oil industry. I was put on diving vessels which, when you think about it, were very close to the Red Sea, so the sea life was amazing! I was also onboard anchor-handling towing vessels which were designed to lift the anchors, then we would connect our towing wire to the rig and tow them to the new location. I worked on a production vessel, taking local day workers to their platforms. I would leave the port at 7am and drop them off, then around 4pm, I would start to pick them all back up and take them to the port. Of course, this only happened when the weather conditions were good. If the sea was rough, the workers would travel by helicopter.

One day, I was on board the vessel and my instruction was to stand by in the Morgan Field, which was close to the Sinai side, and wait to pick up the crew working on one of the platforms. It was about 2am and I was letting the vessel drift, just observing what was around me, when all of a sudden, out of nowhere, a searchlight shone onto me! It was the Israeli navy patrol boat! They called me on the VHF and told me to allow them to come alongside and board!

The first thing that flashed through my mind was that I would be tossed into an Israeli prison cell and the key would be thrown away! I immediately positioned my vessel so that it would make them uncomfortable if they did try to come alongside me. I could see them trying to make a run, then they called it off and proceeded back to their port on the Sinai side.

Between the months of April and October, I would say that 80 per cent of the wind was between 35 and 45 knots, from the north west. We may have got a few days where it was not too bad but usually it was blowing strong sometimes even stronger than 35-45 knots, so strong that certain ports would have to shut down as conditions made it unsafe to keep open.

Then, from October/November through to March, the sea conditions reversed; 80 per cent flat, calm and slight winds from the south east direction. Some say that the Gulf of Suez was like a tunnel for the wind. The Sinai Peninsula was opposite the port we were working from, so if weather conditions became too much, we would head for shelter until it passed.

I was on board one of the company vessels, which was named 'Gulf Fleet 1' and it was a multipurpose vessel, or, I should really say, a maintenance vessel. It was fitted out with two lifting cranes, welding plants and workshops. It was a nice, smallish vessel. Adequate for its designated job.

I think back to the year 1979-1980 and, of course, all the Egyptian assets, especially oil fields, on the Sinai side of the Gulf of Suez were under the control of the Israeli forces. There was one particular field named Shab-Ali ('shab' is the Egyptian name for 'reef' and 'Ali' means high). This was close to Ras Mohamed, which was near Sharm El Sheik; now a booming tourist industry.

The Israeli forces had taken control of this field (and others) and of course, it was just mass production, during the conflict, between the two countries.

My job entailed navigating my ship between the reefs to arrive at the platforms and carry out major repairs on the production platforms. At this time, there were no lights guiding us into the channel in between the reefs, so for safety, it was a case of daylight navigation only. Also, in Shab-Ali, surrounded by the reefs, we would still get the wind, but we had very good protection from the seas, so it was always comfortable weather to work in. I can say that the 'Gulf Fleet 1' was the first vessel hired by the Egyptian people to enter the Shab-Ali field since the Israelis returned the properties.

For me, working there was very tranquil, as there were no facilities for helicopters to land on any of the platforms.

It was interesting, watching the development getting back to normal again.

After a while, when the channel was fixed and lit up with navigation channel buoys, the big, heavy lift crane barge and dive support barges arrived. Their first task was to make the channel bigger, so that the material barges could come and go without waiting, as new pipe lines were to be laid across the Gulf of Suez to the Cairo side of the sea.

So, we sailed back to our port, which was located in the middle of the Gulf of Suez; a small man-made dug-out called Ras Shukeir.

While I was mate of the 'Gulf Fleet 1', we were on standby in the Morgan oil field, which was in the Gulf of Suez, when we received a distress call from a supply vessel using the same port as us. It was called 'Smit Lloyd 10', they were close to the Morgan field and they were sinking! After informing Field Control, we headed towards the stricken vessel.

It was not too far away from us and, thank God, the weather was good. We got close and saw the life rafts in the sea. We manoeuvred up close to them and shouted out, "Is everyone safe?" The answer was "Yes!" However, the master was still on the vessel and she was sinking.

We got close to the 'Smit Lloyd 10' and, by this time, her decks were becoming submerged. The master was on the bridge wing with a briefcase in his hands, containing the ship's documents etc.

We managed to get the master onto our ship and he was in good health, apart from being in shock. Please remember, we knew the master personally.

We proceeded to the life rafts and, of course, by this time, there were lots of other vessels in the vicinity, waiting to see if they could be of any assistance.

We picked all the crew up and led them to the accommodation for checks, drinks etc. Again, thanks to the good Lord, no one had been hurt. We then headed for the port to land the survivors and, before leaving, we saw a supply vessel alongside the sinking ship. They were attempting to put their tow wire on the sinking vessel so that they could claim salvage money. But this was not to be; as soon as the tow wire was connected, the 'Smit Lloyd' started to sink more quickly. We saw the vessel's crew cutting through their tow wire, with oxygen and acetylene for a quick exit, in case they got pulled under the sea.

We arrived back in the port of Ras Shukeir and the authorities came down, including immigration officials etc. The distressed crew members were taken away to have medical checks and then, having lost all their possessions, they had to go to their embassies to obtain new passports in order to be repatriated. So really that was that.

Later on, we sat down and discussed how good it was that no one had lost their life.

So again, we carried on working out of Ras Shukeir. Business was back to normal, or near enough.

This was our base and we would run from this port, up and down the Gulf of Suez, for many years to come.

Later, I was put on a production vessel called the 'Avoyelles'. This was my promotion to skipper, so I was pleased, but in fact no one wanted this boat, as there was no bow thruster, so it was controlled by stern propulsion only. She was a very old boat, belonging to the Egyptian oil company Gupco.

The ship needed a lot of TLC, so I started with that. At that time, we were working a shift patter of three months away and one month off. For me, it was a good project, just to get the vessel in a good shape. Previously, our company had sailed the vessels northward through the Suez Canal to Greece and carried out the dry docking/repairs there, but as time went by, costs came into the equation, and we were docking the vessels at local ports i.e. Suez, Port Said and Ismailia.

I remember when the 'Avoyelles' was sent to Greece for dry dock. I was on holiday and when my holiday was finished, I flew to Piraeus, Greece, to join the vessel. The plan was that she would be in the dock for approximately one month. When I arrived, there was a captain from Gupco, who was their company representative, and his name was Hassan Hafez. I found him to be a very decent chap; nothing was a problem for him.

So the docking operations got underway. My mate was from the same town as me and also was an ex-trawler skipper like myself, so all was good.

The crew and myself were all accommodated onshore in the hotel, and each evening, when we had finished our days' work, we would head back and I would assign one of the deck crew to keep night duty for security.

Once we had been at the shipyard for a while, I decided to bring my wife out for two weeks. I informed the Gupco representative and he said, "Good idea!" Unbeknown to me, Hassan was planning the same thing!

My wife arrived and had brought our two younger children; Lisa, who was about 12 years old and our son, Kenny, who was about 10. It was so strange, as so did Hassan's wife, and their children were similar ages. They were called Mohamed and Ghada, and right from the beginning, the children really got along with each other! I remember that we all had a really good time. Then, after two weeks, my wife and children returned home, as did Hassan's family.

Time went on at the shipyard, but progress was so slow. After a while, I told my wife to come back, so that she could have a more relaxing holiday, which she did.

All things come to an end, and the dockyard had completed the vessel's refurbishment and repairs, so we sailed her back to her home in Ras Shukeir.

We were in and out of the harbour, going to the oil fields and supplying the drilling rigs and production platforms for ongoing work. I was now at a point where I was thinking of moving on and taking on a new 'challenge'.

I had appreciated my time with Gulf Fleet Incorporated, but it was time to move on.

Strangely enough, one day, we were tied up at the dock in Ras Shukeir, when I was approached by the Pan Marine operations manager, whose name was Pee Wee Abshire. I had spoken to Pee Wee many a time, as even when you were in competition, you still respected everyone. I also knew Pee Wee from when he was a captain on the 'Alex Tide'.

Anyhow, Pee Wee was asking me questions; keen to know my thoughts on working with Gulf Fleet. I was wondering what direction this was going in, so I asked, "What's going on, Pee Wee?" Round about this time, I was due leave, so was preparing myself for going home. I also had been informed by the Gulf Fleet operations manager that when we went through Cairo, we would be approached by the boss and told that we had to accept a salary cut! I had worked the finances out and I was going to lose about 20 per cent of my earnings. We were paid in US dollars, so we had to hope that the exchange rate would be good!

So, on with the story! Pee Wee asked me to join his company, in the same place, and become captain on one of his diving vessels! The reason he asked me this was because the divers had been causing quite a few problems and he thought I would be the right man for the job. For me, that was a morale boost! At least someone from outside had been looking in!

He also said to me that when I go to Cairo to go home, I should call in at Pan Marine's office and sign a contract with the area manager. Also, I would be getting a 40 per cent pay increase, so that was really good for me!

So when my relief came on board, I went to the office in Ras Shukeir to discuss the impending pay cut. The operations manager told me it would be a cut of 10 US dollars per day. To me, this was unacceptable.

So, I headed for Cairo and met with the Gulf Fleet manager, who looked at me apologetically. He said he had been instructed by Houston to deduct from all payrolls. He went on and on and on! I asked him, to his face, what the daily cut was, and he said to me, "Ten dollars per day." I just looked at him and said, "I got told it was only five dollars per day!" He was surprised at this comment and then he said, "Oh, OK, that is fine." Immediately afterwards, I told him, "Please accept my resignation." He said, "Why?" So I replied, "You are a liar. This deduction has not come from

Houston, but yourself. If it had come from Houston, ten dollars would be ten dollars; nothing more to say."

He did not know what to say and felt so silly.

The biggest shock I got was when he said, "I know you have had an offer from Pan Marine and I will match it if you stay with us." It disgusted me that they had threatened to cut my salary, then just because I did not back down, were willing to give me a 40 per cent increase! Straight away, I thought, "If this is how this company works, I do not want any part in it."

I just told him, "Thank you, bye bye!"

I left Gulf Fleet office for the UK and the next step on my employment path!

So I moved on to 'pastures green', as they say, and the fun started again.

I was assigned to a vessel called 'Gates Tide' with Tidewater Marine, which was a nice vessel with a four-point anchor mooring system on board, which meant I could manoeuvre the ship and, in turn, drop the four anchors and be in a good, stable position as I carried divers, who would need the vessel to be steady as a rock while they carried out their diving operations.

So I got going with my new company, but as it was in the same place as Gulf Fleet, I kept in touch with my previous working associates, and we kept good relationships up.

When I got on board, the diving superintendent and the diving supervisor met me and introduced themselves. One was British and the other was South African. These divers were ex-North Sea and supposedly the *creme de la creme*. They were working for a company called W and W; Whartons and Williams. The South African chap would be with me on the vessel, and the other chap would be based shore side, which I thought was fine.

154

Running the vessel, we were considered the 'work horse', as sometimes we would be anchored up on a four point mooring, while the divers were gas diving (deeper depths) and other times, we would be engaged in rig moves, to make sure the spud cans were being placed on the seabed correctly, so we barely came into the port of Ras Shukeir, which was not too bad.

I must admit, there were a lot of ups and downs on the vessel; especially working with divers, as they were considered to be quite aggressive! They were referred to as such from day one, and after working with them, I didn't disagree with the description!

I remember the trials and tribulations I had with the divers; especially the supervisor. I must admit that towards the end, we did eventually become 'friends', but it was so difficult!

One time, we had left the port of Ras Shukeir and the supervisor was on the bridge with me, just chatting about the job etc. while the rest of my crew and his were preparing equipment etc. for the job we were going to.

My vessel was contracted out to the local company known as Gupco, therefore all inter-vessel activity was fine, provided everyone was working for the same client i.e. Gupco. Anyhow, the diving supervisor said to me that on our way to our destination, we had to rendezvous with another dive vessel to give them some equipment. I said that was fine, assuming they would be working for the same client.

When we approached the other vessel, the diving companies were the same, but the client was different, so I told the supervisor, "Sorry, no can do, as this is conspiracy with the competition and I am not doing it." Well, that man hit the roof! He was screaming at me, the master of the vessel. He said I would not work again etc. If this had been on the television, it would have been good viewing! I just looked at him and treated him with the contempt he deserved.

He said he wanted to use the ship's radio to call his boss onshore and I refused to let him. Again, he went off. I knew that he was about to get violent with me, and he was also quite a few years younger, but I stood my ground. In the end, I told him to leave the bridge, and he did. By this time, we were approaching our job site.

I secured the vessel and everything was prepared for the diving operations. Then I saw the diving supervisor throw his arms out and he must have said something like, "We are not going to do the job," which was not a problem for me, as I had secured the vessel, so my part of the operation was complete!

I sat on the sofa in the bridge, pondering whys and what fors, then who should come back to the bridge, but the diving supervisor! I immediately told him, "You are banned from the bridge."

He came forward and sat next to me on the sofa and said, "Ken, why is it like this?" I just looked at him and said, "Because you made it like this." He put his arm around me and just broke down in tears. What could I say? He said he just wanted us to have a good working relationship and I told him we had, until he started thinking he was better than anyone else and I had to bring him back to reality. It is true, the saying, "you have to be cruel to be kind."

After a while, we shook hands and decided to put the past in the past and move on.

But there were other exciting moments yet to come!

My relief was an American chap and he was decent, but of course I had never sailed with him. I came back to the ship after a holiday and I saw that the captain was bruised and had a cut on his face. He told me the story; the ship had been in Ras Shukheir, so the dive crew had gone onshore to 'socialise'. Consequently, they had got too drunk and shouting had turned into a brawl. No matter what happens, no one on any vessel has the right to strike the captain; it is classed as a form of mutiny. So, when this arises, it is a bad situation, and arise it had.

The captain went off the ship for his holidays. I remember that all the storm doors throughout the ship had, fixed near to them, what we call a 'dogging down bar'; basically a small length of pipe fitted on a bracket on the door for easy access. When you wanted to close the door, this bar would help you get more leverage to make it watertight.

So, I decided to utilise one! I put a whipping on the end (a nice rope handle, which could be passed through to my wrist; similar to a policeman's truncheon, except this was made of steel!)

As I was sitting in my chair on the bridge and we were steaming along, the diving supervisor came to the bridge and we were idly chatting. Then he saw my bar and asked me what it was for. I told him that if he ever thinks he can assault a captain, especially me, he is welcome. I looked him straight in the eye and told him, "If I ever, for one minute, think that you are acting stupid, I will have no hesitation in hitting you across your bald head." (He was bald as a balloon, but still a lot younger than me).

So time went by, and the relationship between myself and the diving supervisor was, I would say, 'fragile'.

There was another 'incident' while we were alongside in Ras Shukeir, waiting for orders and for weather conditions to ease.

It was evening time and the dive crew had gone onshore to their base camp. I was just relaxing in my cabin. I was awake but getting ready to go to sleep.

Just before midnight, when I was in my bed, I heard all the divers coming back and it sounded hectic, to say the least! I was already 'wound up' like spring, in view of the past incidents, but I am a fair man and I did appreciate that the environment we were working. . . well, I suppose they needed to 'chill out' now and then!

Anyhow, they all bundled into the mess room on the main deck level and I could hear the noise, which was at a very high decibel!

Now I was beginning to lose my composure, but I stayed in my bed. I could tell that the expats had consumed quite a bit of alcohol, and there were a couple of them making the bullets for the diving supervisor to fire.

While they had been onshore, being an experienced offshore captain, I told the cook to leave a cold buffet out for them, then lock everything up and give me the key. Consequently, the divers were egging the diving supervisor on to come to my cabin and get the food stores key so that they could have a whopping 'fry-up'. Of course, like a chump, the diving supervisor agreed and I heard him struggling up the stairs to my cabin. My cabin was in absolute darkness, then the door was flung open and all I could hear was something like, "Capshan, capshan, gish me the key!"

I kept the light off and just spoke these few words to the diving supervisor: "Tony, you have two choices: you can either keep walking into my cabin and suffer the consequences, or you can turn around, go back, and everything will be forgotten."

He froze, started jabbering about something, then did a 180 degree turn out of my cabin and went back to the mess room.

Feeling smug and relaxed, I rolled over and had a good night's sleep.

The following morning, yes, heads did roll, and the dive team never forgot that incident!

I spent about three years on the dive boat and lots of expats came and went during my time there. Yes, we did have problems, but they all got ironed out. I even remember receiving a Christmas card from the diving supervisor once he had returned to his native country (he was of South African origin).

When the vessel's dry-docking survey came up, I would sail it through the Suez Canal to a port called Ismailia, and they would get us up into the dry dock, repair our faults and prepare the vessel for returning to Ras Shukeir to continue our work with Gupco.

Regarding our company's management in Cairo, I was reasonably OK with them, and the manager said that when I went to Ismailia, I should invite my wife to Egypt.

Jean arrived in Cairo and was met by the company. They put us up in the International Continental which, at that time, was a five star, and yes it was very nice. We stayed there for three days, then we were driven up to Ismailia and stayed in another nice hotel. Each day, I would be able to check how the work was going, then join my wife back at the hotel, and we would go around the places in Ismailia. Yes, it was good.

When you are in the shipyard, you tend to get close to people, as you are working with them each and every day. The management in the Ismailia dockyard were good people, and one day, they invited my wife and myself to a 'garden party'. I must say that my wife is rather nervous and hesitant when it comes to going to random houses and accepting food from strangers!

Well, we popped along and all the local wives and other females really made my wife welcome, but the local foods were very different! The most surprising part of it all was that we were invited to go on board one of the Egyptian Navy vessels! There we were, steaming up and down the Suez Canal, passing all the ships! It was something to remember.

My time in Egypt was coming to an end, I felt. Also Ras Shukeir, our base, was starting to get a bit over the top with situations. So, I posted a request for a transfer out of Egypt, which was accepted, so I knew things would be changing soon.

In the meantime, I was transferred to a smaller base port, just a little away from Ras Shukeir, which was called Ras Gharib, to work for Total, a French company. I spent months with them, waiting for my transfer.

In 1988, I got my transfer! The next place would be Bombay (now Mumbai) and, again, I was going to pastures new!

My company was going into a joint venture with the Indian Government and there were going to be at least 15 vessels. This was very good; at least we would be there in force! But, as you will see, things rarely turn out as you planned or expected.

At that time, the Indian Government (I think they called themselves IEOC) was constructing an oil and gas supply base at a place called Navara, but at that time, we were still working from a commercial dock called Victoria.

I did learn a lot and I still say that we all learn something new every day! My first experience came when we were at the dockside. The vessel I had joined had come from West Africa. It was called 'Ramy Tide' and on the deck, there were loads of odds and sods, plus a fibre glass boat with an outboard motor. We had our original lifesaving boats in place, so this one was surplus to requirement.

We asked the dock master if there was a place onshore for us to stow it as, bear in mind, the three vessels which had arrived were the forerunners for the company, so, in reality, we had no storage area for spares. Anyhow, the dock master said that he did not have any room, even though the dockyard area was massive. There was clearly some wheeling and dealing going on; the dock master wanted this boat for himself.

Our manager stood his ground and said, in front of the dock master, "Captain, take the boat back to your ship and do what you like with it. Keep it on board, sell it, give it to fishermen or even sink it." Things had got off to a rocky start; time would tell if the future would be good and beneficial to our company.

We sailed to the rig and did the work, coming back with cargos from the rig which were to be landed onshore, and then, out of the blue, came a call from our agent that we could not proceed alongside to the dock, as we did not have the necessary paperwork! I was amazed.

So, we anchored up in the river and, of course, our manager knew the story. He got on a river taxi and came on board. We had a discussion and it was so ridiculous that the operator had taken the vessel off hire, as we had his property on board, and I had always been told that all the time you have property of the operator on board, you will never be off hire!

The politics involved were so pathetic.

We were anchored in the 'Bombay roads' for about five days. It was a shame that the industry worked like that. During this time, we decided to clean out the bulk tanks (which were below decks, but accessible from the deck, and filled with cement and barite in dry powder form).

To put it bluntly, it was a hell of a job to clean those tanks out! The manager organised a cleaning gang from shore (all locals, may I add), and when they came on board via a small boat, there must have been at least 30 of them! They just stripped down to their shorts and got stuck; shovelling it out and relaying in into buckets. It was a very demanding task!

People were working shifts. Those finishing at 6pm would hose themselves down with our freshwater hose, eat our leftovers, find themselves a piece of cardboard, lie down on that and go to sleep for the night. I really did feel sorry for them, and I expect that they got paid little more than nothing.

Then we were back up and running and life carried on. My relief arrived in Bombay and told me I could not be relieved at sea (which was untrue, as when I arrived, I boarded the ship at sea, so to me, this was just a reason not to go offshore).

I ended up doing 21 days over my contracted time and was so disgusted with the operation that I said I would not return. The company said it would be better next time etc. but I had heard the same song many times before, so I decided to look elsewhere.

When I got home, I told my wife that I would like to try something different. I had heard of an oil rig company in Aberdeen and thought I might have a chance of a job. I called the company, which was called Odeco, and they set up an interview with the marine manager.

So, on the day of the interview, in the early hours of the morning, the two of us set off for Aberdeen. It was a long drive, (seven hours), and we arrived around midday. I went for my interview while Jean had a look around the shops.

The interview went well, but there has always been a barrier between merchant Navy personnel and fishermen. Merchant Navy people tend to look down on fishermen; why, I do not know, as fishermen are the backbones of the industry and have the most dangerous occupation.

So I sat there, listening to this ex-Navy person, who was just rabbiting on about things etc.

After two hours of this and that, I got the job as a BCO (ballast control operator).

I met back with my wife and we had some lunch, then headed back home; another seven hours!

I joined a rig called 'Ocean Kokuwei', which was in the stacked mode (no contract) with minimal crew on board, just to keep things running. I introduced myself to the OIM (offshore installation manager) who seemed OK, as did the crew in general.

Anyhow, I received a job description, listing what was expected of me, and so I started working.

After a while, at Inver Gordon, it was becoming quite boring, so I decided to clean out and tidy up the propulsion rooms. These were situated at the very bottom deck of the rig. The place was a dump; no one had really taken care of it! So this was my task for the next two weeks on board.

In the propulsion rooms, there were actuators with copper lines running out. This system was for ballasting the rig down, with the seawater pumping system. I decided to change all the lines in one of the rooms for new ones. I also cleaned and painted the room and, to be honest, I was very impressed with my work!

The OIM came down and complimented me on my work, saying I had done a great job, then made the comment, "Ken. . . don't think that your relief will do the other propulsion room when you go on holiday," and I thought, "It seems like anyone can do as they please!" So my response was, "No problem. I will have something to do when I come back after leave."

I had a nice two weeks' leave, then the company said that while the rig was in Inver Gordon, I would go to Robert Gordon Institute in Aberdeen to sit my offshore survival course.

So off I went, back to Aberdeen, and after five days, I had finished and was ready to go back to 'Ocean Kokuwei' in Inver Gordon. I had been staying at the Station Hotel in Aberdeen, which was just across the road from the train station, which was very handy for catching the train to Inver Gordon.

The rig manager called me and said that before going to the rig, I had to 'swing by' the office to pick up manuals for the rig, plus a couple more for other Odeco rigs in Inver Gordon. I was not impressed, so I asked him if one of the office staff could drop them off at my hotel, and then I could just walk across the road to the station. Well, he kicked off and said all manner of nasty swear words to me!

I was angry, but the rig manager was big and could have blown me away, so the following morning, I went to our office (via taxi) and picked up this big bundle of manuals. Then I took the taxi back to the train station. I asked the taxi driver how much the fare was, and then I told him to return to the office we had just been at and ask for the rig manager, Willy, and get the money from him. So off he went.

No more to be said, I struggled to get on the train with my bags and manuals, but eventually got to the rig.

A few days later, the rig manager paid us a visit and I was standing on the deck. Talk about red rag to a bull! He came charging at me on the deck and we were nose to nose. I thought he was going to throw me in the dock! Then he went on about the taxi fare and everything. I just told him that if he didn't like it, he could fire me! He was not too impressed with my answer!

The funny thing was, during my time with Odeco, each time I travelled to and from the rig, I would pop in to my old company, Tidewater, who had an office in Regent's Quay, Aberdeen. They would say, "David Smiley (the area manager) has a job for you, Ken," but I would politely decline.

Anyhow, time went on, the rig got a contract to work and away we went to the location.

Once there, we started drilling etc. and I went home and came back several times, but eventually we finished the job. Then it was back to our old haunt, Inver Gordon. I just have to put this small piece in . . . during my stay with Odeco, because I had refurbished the propulsion rooms (sorting out the actuators, air lines etc.) the company sent me on a 'special' job to Bay of Biscay, to one of the company's other rigs. I was there to be a mechanic, as none of their ballasting systems were working, and they needed the system up and running. Myself, I was never a mechanically-minded person, so being sent on this job seemed a little unreal!

I arrived on the rig along with another 'mechanic' and we got stuck into repairing the system. The rig was full of people, as they were in the drilling mode. Consequently, the OIM approached us and said that there were no cabins available for my friend and I, and could we go down to the standby vessel each night and sleep there. So, we would be working on the rig during the day and sleeping on the vessel at night. Well, I kicked off. I said it was dangerous, going down to the vessel; the sea was rough, I would be seasick etc. (Please remember; all my life I had been on the sea, so I was just being a little difficult, as I thought we were not getting treated properly for the job we had come out to do!) The OIM said he would put us on treble overtime pay, so we agreed.

We went down to the ship and the steward met us and showed us to our cabin. We had our evening meal and it was like paradise, compared to the rig conditions! It was perfect. That was how things were until the job was completed.

Then, I returned to the 'Ocean Kokuwei' and we were coming into Inver Gordon. By that point, I had completed 12 months with the company, but I was still not happy with the job.

We left the rig and on the dockside was an office delegate who was handing out redundancy forms. He was calling names out and as the motto was, 'last in, first out', I knew I would be one of them.

He called my name and as I stepped forward, he said, "Oh no, sorry; they have another job for you," and I said, "No, thank you," as I wanted the redundancy form so that I could maybe claim some tax relief.

I left Inver Gordon feeling OK with myself, as I knew I had my old company to fall back on, going back to the anchor-handling vessels.

When I arrived at the Tidewater office at Regent's Quay, Aberdeen, and told them I was available for work, they said, "Oh, all is quiet here. There's nothing happening, regarding work!"

At that moment, I just felt terrible. Then, out of the blue, the manager said, "Don't worry Ken; we will send you a contract to sign. Just make sure you don't go wandering off with anyone else!" I thought that was very nice of them and I headed home.

I got my contract through the post and, to be fair, anything was better than nothing, but I rang the Aberdeen office up and said that I could not sign the contract, as the day rate was not enough!

So they said, "OK, we will increase the rate," and I was pleased with my contract negotiating!

I woke up the following morning to the phone ringing. It was the Odeco rig manager; the one who I had been nose to nose with, arguing. He said, "Ken, I want you to go on the 'Ocean Liberator'". I spoke nicely and said, "Willy thank you so much for the job offer, but it is not for me. I will go back to the boats." I did recommend my son-in-law for the job, but the manager didn't accept, so really that was me and Odeco abruptly finished.

This was the first time I had been unemployed in many years, so I thought I would see what the unemployment office could do to help me. The system was awful, and, in the end, I just told the lady, "OK, that's fine. I will not bother. Thank you; I will find a job myself."

I went home feeling very let down with the system.

When I got home, my contract had arrived from Tidewater, and it was not all that good, so I returned it for better terms. It came back a few days later with a higher rate on it, so that was good for me.

I was sitting at home when the phone rang. It was a representative from the Dubai division of Tidewater. They asked me if I would go there to run a four-point mooring dive vessel out of Doha in Qatar. They quoted me a daily rate and I told them I would contact them soon.

I got in touch with my office in Aberdeen and they told me that if the rate was higher, I should go, as when it was completed, I would come back home for ten days, then on to Brazil.

So all was agreed and off I went to Dubai, then on to Doha in Qatar, where I stayed for approximately one month.

The job was OK and, of course, there will always be one who has to try and prove something, but I just treated it with the contempt it deserved.

I remember that, when we entered and departed the port, no matter what time of day or night, all the crew would have to gather on the dockside for immigration to check.

I thought this was not too good, as a lot of people were asleep or resting, so I went to the immigration team and started speaking in Arabic (I had learned this in Egypt) and they were so amazed that they agreed not to disturb any of the crew on board, so at least I achieved something worthwhile.

We sailed and there was a small offshore base at this place called Das Island, and we used to pull in there for fuel, water etc.

I did my time and my relief came out to Das Island. After handing over, I jumped on a vessel coming back to Doha, arrived in port and flew back home. That was my little stint in Doha completed; now to prepare for Brazil.

I flew down to Brazil and, straight away, I was not too impressed, as the company said, "You must learn Portuguese." Not 'try', but 'must'! So, I got myself a travel book and CD to try and learn some local language.

I arrived in Rio and was transported to my assigned vessel, which was called 'Mammoth Tide'. She was laid at the dock, undergoing certain replacements, then she would be ready to go on hire for Petrobras, an oil company.

Something inside me told me that this was not a good place to be. No one was even trying to speak English, and my chief mate, who was Yugoslavian, seemed not to be interested in anything at all. So I thought, "You are on your own again, Ken!"

The good thing was that the operation manager was Pee Wee Abshire, whom I had worked in Egypt with, and he was a sound chap. He took me to the office one day and as we stepped out of the lift, there were two of the biggest men I have ever seen! They were guarding the office, and each had a sawn-off shot gun laid across their arms. It was a scary sight!

Later, I got taken back to the ship to get acclimatised to the vessel etc.

As time went by, Pee Wee left and was replaced by Geerd; a Dutchman who was not my type. He lived in Rio, so basically, he was a 'local chap'.

The time came when all of our jobs had been completed. We would come back on hire with Petrobras Brazil, as it seemed like, prior to me joining the vessel, she had been working in West Africa and was returning to Brazil.

Well, on this particular day, this truck rolls up, full of alcohol and with food fit for a five-star hotel! I was amazed at the amount and the quality. The port captain (Geerd) followed down and all this stuff was loaded onto the ship, into the recreation room and galley. The port captain explained that this was a little party for the fiscal! The fiscal was, of course, the Petrobras personnel, who wanted everything for nothing, presents etc. I was new to the area, but it was a case of same idea, different place!

The port captain said that they would board us from seaward, from the pilot boat or something similar, and he also said that my crew would line up on the deck in new coveralls to meet the fiscal coming on board, with me at the head of the line. I immediately told the port captain that if I were a manager of a football club, then I would do that, but he had the wrong man here. The port captain was very disappointed with my response but accepted it.

Anyhow, they all came on board (about 10 people) ate, drank and went away merry. I didn't feel good about the full setup here.

We eventually got on hire and away we sailed to the field to work with the rigs and platforms. We were running 24/7 and there were quite a few vessels scattered around. After a while, we sailed back to the Port of Macae. It was a busy place, and regardless of the cargos etc. you stayed in port no more than eight hours. So, for our crew changes, food provisions etc. we had to have our planning spot-on, as you sailed whether you had what you needed or not!

We got back to the field and were on call for a rig move. I thought that was fine, but in the meantime, they were running us all over the place, transferring cargo etc. which, for me, was ridiculous, as my crew needed rest prior to the rig move operation. I just got fed up with the system and everything and dropped the anchor so we could rest. To say the least, there was quite a bit of conversation about this, but I didn't know about it until I woke the following morning. My company was not too impressed, but I am sorry to say there was no organisation at all.

We commenced operations again and did the rig move, and on my next visit to the port, I went to see the port authorities, to discuss changing our port call schedule, as every time I steamed about the fields, I could see local vessels just on standby, doing nothing.

When I approached the local in charge, he just looked at me and said, "You, Gringo" and for me that spoke volumes. So I left the building, without so much as a by your leave. I was not impressed with the Brazilian system at all. I thought, "Just do the job and get out." I was coming up for my relief time and was in daily contact with our office, which was based in Rio De Janeiro, and the work site was in Macae, so it would take about three hours by car or bus to get here.

The office told me that the relief was on his way but, of course, after four hours; still no show. I was so upset. I had my bag all ready and on the dockside. I told the office that the relief had better make it, as if not, the vessel would be off hire as I would not sail it.

Eventually, he did turn up and, of course, it turns out he was a friend of the management! I handed over then pushed off to Rio by bus and got to the rest house in Rio. The operation manager came to visit and he had my flight ticket with him.

I looked on the ticket and it said 'return'! Of course, I pointed this out to him and he said, "Oh yes; when you have had some time off, you will want to return." I told him he was a silly person, as when I say "No", that is what it means.

So I headed home, and that was my work experience with Brazil completed, thank you very much!

I was home on leave and enjoying my time off with my wife and family. We had nice holidays and I am pleased we had our children with us all the time.

I got a call from the Aberdeen office when my nice leave was coming to an end, and I was assigned to Israel.

I got to Heathrow Airport. Going through security checks, I had to go back at least four times as they were so strict! Anyhow, I finally landed in Tel Aviv, then went on to a port called Ashdod, and finally on board the ship, which was called 'Sirio Tide'. It was a good ship; about 6000 hp which, at that time, was not too bad, and I knew our contract would be finishing in a few weeks.

I was alongside the dock at Ashdod, and I heard cockney voices as I sat in my cabin. I found out the people were from immigration, and they would board us on each entry and exit from the port. They told me they were all English, but of Jewish descent. So they would get called back to serve their time in one of the country's forces i.e., Air Force, Army etc. It was interesting to listen to them talk, and they enjoyed going back to their roots. They were nice people.

It was a very tense area to work in, as the rig we serviced was a dynamic drill ship, so at short notice, they could unlatch from the drill string at the seabed and just steam away. They did a few times, when we received possible terror alerts. That was something we did not want for sure. The Israelis were very thorough and protective of themselves.

After a few weeks, we had finished the contract with Israel and my order was to steam to Portugal for dry docking. They would update me with more information at a later date.

We were steaming along the Mediterranean Sea towards Portugal, and the weather was nice; typical spring weather. We were approaching Italy and I received a message to proceed to Sardinia; no mention of what the job would be, the time it would take or anything. So I was completely in the dark. Anyhow, as instructed, I proceeded to the west coast of Sardinia to a port called Oristano.

With this being my first time in Sardinia, I adjusted my speed, to make sure I arrived at the pilot station at first light of day. I called the port authorities to inform them of my arrival and they told me that the pilot was underway to me, so that was fine. I had all my documents ready to be seen by the port authorities.

At daylight, I spotted a small fishing boat chugging towards me. I was informed that he was the pilot and was instructed to follow him, which I did, before tying up at the dockside.

Up to this point, I had been involved in the oil and gas industries, but that was about to change.

The port of Oristano was of a good size, as it was a large commercial port. I knew the water would be a good depth, so that was fine with me.

The first chap to come on board was representing customs and immigration. He inspected the bonded stores etc. then passports, so all that was good. At this time, the majority of my crew were Yugoslavians, and they were good.

So yes, that part was completed; bearing in mind I still didn't have a clue what our job was going to be!

The chap left the vessel and when he returned, he said he was our agent for clearance etc. so, again, that was good, and the chap (who was Italian, of course) was really sociable. So it seemed that this chap was into everything, and it would make my job easier. Then, after all the coming and going, he stepped back on board and finally said to me that he was the client! I was taken aback, as this man had covered all parts of the vessel's entry and work scope, so yes, he was really involved! Then he told me, "We will hold a meeting in a couple of days, regarding our expectations," which I looked forward to.

True to his word, the client/agent came on board, followed by a party of gentlemen; some of whom were wearing service uniforms! I was astounded, but when they got close, I realised that the service personnel were high-ranking officers from the USA Air Force.

I must admit; they were very relaxed and really easy to converse with! So that was the operation; the US Air Force had marine buoys anchored to the seabed in various positions offshore, and it was time for the securing system to be renewed, as the buoys had been anchored for four years. They explained to me that they would never have another situation like Vietnam, so what they did here, through NATO, was to install computers in the buoys, and then the plane pilots would do target practice with this system; hence the training would be perfect. (Please remember; it was the 1980s, and from then, things would change in the world, so these fighters had to be ready for combat).

I must say that our agent/client apparently owed all the beaches around the port of Oristano and yes, the beaches were full of tourists, so he employed his son as an assistant, and he was also in charge of the lifeguards. His son was funny; each day, he would say to his father, in front of me, "Father, I want to be a millionaire like you," and his father's response was, "Get off your backside and earn it, like I did!" So he was really down to earth, in that respect.

So we loaded up our equipment and the strange thing was that the mooring buoy was not secured to the seabed with chain or wire, which is normal, but with plaited nylon rope. I knew, through my own experience, that this was difficult to splice, but here, the finished splice had to look good. An American joined us, who specialised in this kind of rope splicing.

So we set sail and it took six hours to reach our first change-out operation. The weather was very good and the sea calm, which made life easier and safer. It made a nice change that the job wasn't oil or gas related.

We were connected to the buoy and prepared all the equipment for the work. By that time, it was coming to the end of the day, and as it was such a delicate job, it was only conducted in daylight hours.

So that was the end of the first day, and I sat on the bridge wing that evening with a cup of tea, watching the Mediterranean Sea and the sun slowly setting in the west. Life was good.

The next morning, I got the buoy onto our deck and secured the mooring rope so that we were well-secured while the buoy was disconnected. The water depth was approximately 1600 metres (just about a mile) which was very deep.

We started to heave in the old mooring line (which had been attached for four years) and it was amazing, seeing all the plankton living on the rope; all different types of insect-looking sea life, scurrying about. It was unbelievable.

On our deck, we had lots of containers, which held the new nylon mooring ropes. Each mooring system had three nylon ropes to the anchor from the buoy, which needed replacing. The American chap would show us his skills with the rope, and I must admit, he was very good at his job! We had to be vigilant, but when it was smooth sailing, we could go ahead changing out the ropes.

We stowed all the old ropes (which were still in good condition) in the open containers, so that we had a safe working deck and could avoid any accidents/incidents.

The entire operation took six weeks, then we sailed back into the Port of Oristano. When we got back to the port for the final off hire contract, everyone involved in the project was very pleased with our performance, as they thought it would take us longer! So yes, everyone was happy. Also, my company had scheduled us to go to dry dock in Portugal, so that was something to look forward to.

We stayed overnight at the port and I let some of the crew go onshore for some relaxation time, as they had all worked hard, including in very high temperatures, so they deserved it.

I prepared the navigation charts for the next voyage, which would take us to Portugal, then I went sleep.

I woke up the following morning feeling very refreshed and looking forward to our trip to Portugal. I went down to the crew's mess and all was good and ready to go. We received our clearance, and everyone bade us safe sailing.

So watches were set and away we went! We got clear of Sardinia and settled down. The weather was still good, so all was fine on board. Then, not long afterwards, the bubble burst as we got instructions from our head office to cancel the Portugal docking, and instead of turning right at Gibraltar, turn left to Africa! To say this took the wind out of my sails would be a gross understatement. Yet that was my order. We were instructed to sail for a port called

Dakar in Senegal. This would be my first time on the west coast of Africa.

When I think back, the majority of the crew on board were Yugoslavian. Well, they were not too impressed, and quite rightly so, as I was feeling the same. So it did put some strain on the atmosphere on board.

My instruction was to contact our local agent, who would make all docking arrangements etc. so that was not a problem. There would also be an American port engineer who would be in charge of the dry docking, which was expected to take about four weeks.

So off we went, southward.

We arrived at Dakar and it was a good-sized commercial port with large dry-docking yards. One thing I forgot to add is that, when we altered course from the Mediterranean to head down south, I had never seen so many fishing vessels in my life! I remember, at the start of my life, I was used to congested fishing areas, but what I saw surpassed this! They were all different sizes; Spanish vessels and Russian. We were a fair distance from land, so the water they were fishing in was pretty deep.

We eventually arrived at the pilot station off Dakar and the pilot came on board to assist me in entering the dock. He also requested, on completion of securing the vessel, a present! I was the master of the vessel, not Father Christmas! Also, our company had never approved of that policy.

Anyhow, we were secured alongside, waiting for the dry dock to become available, and we started making preparations. Then we got our clearance. The customs had been on board along, with our agent, and he had got some shore passes for the crew, so all was good.

That evening, just before the sun went down, I got a bit of a shock, as a fishing vessel came straight into the harbour, pulled his nets on deck, then went away, back to the open sea. I was a bit shocked, as what he did was illegal, and yet no authority called him or attempted to board the fishing vessel. I was left wondering, "What goes on here?"

The next morning, the company's port engineer came on board. I only remember his first name, which was Jerry. No disrespect, but to look at him, you would think he was looking for hand-outs.

The dry dock work mainly happened in the engine room, so I thought he would be more involved with the chief engineer than with me, so that was not too bad.

We were waiting to enter the dry dock, which we knew would take a few days, when, one evening, when I was sitting in the crew's mess, having a cup of tea, the agent came on board and told all the crew to be careful, as people had been wandering about in the dark. Of course, we kept a gangway watch, so all was controlled there. The agent and I went to the bridge, as he said he wanted to show me something. When we got there, he just pointed, and I saw what he meant. A Russian trawler had entered the dock and I saw lots of trucks loading things, as well as fuel lines. The agent told me that they were stealing things to sell, and that all the crew members got a cut of the proceeds. Never had I seen things move so fast!

I told our crew that if they could get a good price for the nylon rope in the containers, they should sell it, and share the money equally among themselves. They agreed and I left them to it. They sold it for a good price.

We were working with a small barge called 'Alligator' off Point Noire. We went in to the port to do the crew changes and I remember I was in this small pickup, one of the company's trucks, when all of a sudden, there were gunshots everywhere! I squatted on the floor and it stopped just as suddenly. It was deathly quiet. Later on, we found out it had been an attempted coup! So, at the end of it all, I was really glad to be on my way home for some rest!

I arrived home and had about four weeks' leave. Then I was called by the office and asked if I would be interested in working from Brunei. I told them I would be. The trip would be two months on and one off, which sounded good.

So off I went to Brunei.

When I arrived, it seemed that the hotels were fully occupied, so it was arranged that I would stay in a 'boarding house'. The driver dropped me off, then I entered this wooden house on stilts, and a very old man and lady welcomed me in. They could not speak one word of English, and I couldn't speak Malaysian, so there were lots of head movements going on (up and down for yes and across for no). They showed me to my bedroom and gave me a cup of tea. The place was clean and comfortable.

I went to sleep, and they knocked on my door the next morning with a cup of tea and invited me for breakfast. There were boiled eggs, toast with jam and also cereal, which was much appreciated.

The driver arrived and took me down to the supply boat base. Before I boarded the vessel, I had to meet with the Shell Marine Department, just to make sure I wasn't a raving lunatic (or words to that effect).

After the meeting, I was taken to my ship, which was called the 'Bulan Malai' (a local name). The vessel had been purpose-built for Shell Brunei, a Dutch oil company. It was a 'construction vessel', and I would have to approach fixed platforms and drop two bow anchors, go back down to the platform and secure the stern to the platform, and then we would erect a gangway from the stern of the ship to the platform, so that the ship's construction crew could work on the platform. After the day's shift, all would go back to the ship for meals and accommodation.

That was basically the ship's duties. But when I got on board, I found out that one of the main engines was down, so we prepared for a voyage to Singapore to repair/replace the ship's main engine. This was uneventful, and we were soon back in Brunei (south China seas), working with Shell.

The ship was not looking too good cosmetically, and I am a hands-on person, so I got the crew together and told them what needed to be done. So, we made the plan. At this time, I must say, I was a little upset, as each morning, the operation manager would call in and ask for daily progress, and I found out that the chief engineer (Wally, from Australia) was the one who spoke and not the radio man, which was customary. I got the feeling I was being treated as an outcast, rather than the captain of the ship. I gritted my teeth and thought, "My time will come." I was realising that the manager had his own little circle of informants etc. Anyhow, I would deal with this situation at a later stage!

When we went to port (we did 28 days at sea and two back in the port for stores, bunkers and crew changes), I got stuck in with the cleaning and repainting of the vessel. Of course, I was leading by example. I would put on my PPE (Personal Protective Equipment), get on deck with the crew and do my bit. Then, when I went back inside to the bridge, back to my own environment, I would relax and slip into shorts, a t-shirt and sandals, as one does in high-climate countries.

I must admit that the ship was looking good, and the Shell operator was very impressed with the facelift! The crew, too, had a good attitude.

We carried a total of 55 persons; a mixture of nationalities. We had two galleys and mess rooms; one eastern, one western, so there was no chance of arguments.

The Shell company man we carried on board was a British chap, ex-forces, and he was just not my type at all. He was a sneak and always complaining about something, so we just did not see eye to eye.

The construction manager was employed by my company, so we had something in common. He was not a bad chap. Easy to get along with.

I must say, at this stage, that my son (now in his late twenties) was also on board. He was engaged as chief officer and did a very good job. He carried out his duties very well and got on with everyone, so all was good. The sad thing is that, a month after we arrived on board the 'Bulan Malai' together, Shell realised that we were father and son and insisted my son sign off, as this was against company policy. I was OK with this as he had got some overseas experience, and it would be good for him to go home for a rest; especially with the humid weather, which he was not used to.

I knew there was some skulduggery going on with the company man. He was due to leave for his days off, and it seemed he wanted to stir up a lot of trouble with anyone about anything.

We were secured at a platform, and the company man went up to the helideck, waiting for the helicopter. I knew it was not correct behaviour, but my thoughts got the better of me, and I went down to the company man's office and looked through his handover book. Lo and behold, he had made a comment for his relief, which was, "Keep an eye on the captain, as he wanders around the decks without any PPE", which was a complete untruth! I was so angry with this remark, as I had been doing what was best for everyone.

Again, I had the feeling that people were going through the back door and doing childish things. I would have appreciated someone having the decency to confront me with their issues, but unfortunately, it did not work like that.

So, the other company man came on board and he seemed a decent chap. I carried on my duties to the best of my abilities and let the rest of them whistle Dixie, as they say.

Each morning, the AB (seaman) on duty would hoist the flags; the ship's country of registry and the flag of the country you were working in. These two flags were flown during daylight and lowered at dusk.

The seamen were local, so all was fine there, regarding their regulations (or so I thought).

I was in my office one day when a local visitor from the oil company came on board. He was ranting and raving in his own language. Of course, I wanted to know what he was on about. Then it came to my attention that a crew member had turned the Brunei flag upside down! The man had reason to be angry, and he threatened to take me to prison, which I do believe he was in the right position to do. I turned around to the chap and told him that it was one of his countrymen who had done this to his national flag, so if anyone was going to prison, it would be him and not me. He went as quiet as a mouse and just scurried away. Nothing more was said on the subject.

So, we stayed in the field for 28 days, then returned to Brunei to Maura Port, which was our base port. We were allowed two days off hire to get work done, change the crew etc. Our company's marine manager came on board with some managers from Shell, and he was over the moon with the improvement to the vessel's condition. I invited him to my cabin and locked the door, then told him that if he ever made me look stupid again, it would be the last thing he ever did. I was still fuming about him snubbing me on the radio during daily reporting.

I ripped into him big time. He was a disgrace as a manager; he was smelling of alcohol at 9am! I really surprised him and told him to be careful in the future, as he could come down a lot quicker than he went up.

So that was one hurdle finished with! We shook hands before the manager left the ship, so that there would be no ill feeling later. Personally, I was satisfied, as I had sorted the issue once and for all. After that, the manager would always ask for me on the radio, so job done!

Well, I felt a bit better with myself. The crew were working on the deck and the construction crew were doing their business, so I decided to sit and just relax on the bridge.

After a short while, this gentleman came on board and introduced himself as one of the construction team who worked for Shell on the projects. He seemed pleasant enough, asking me questions and for my opinions on things. He then saw my copy of the *Hull Daily Mail* and asked who it belonged to. It was mine, and when he asked if he could take it away with him, I told him, "No problem."

Then it all came out; this chap was born on Hessle Road (as I was) and his brothers, Mike and Dave Patterson, were in the fishing industry. I knew both and had sailed with one, so then we started talking about things back home. This chap had been living in Australia and was pleased to speak to someone from his 'home town'.

He asked me if all was fine, work-wise, and I did mention the run-in I'd had with one of the company men who was based on my vessel. He said, "Don't worry, I will sort it," and after that, I never had that nasty company man reside on my vessel again!

I stayed in Brunei up until 1992, and then moved back to Singapore, which was the head region. We were based at Loyang, and it was a strange set-up, as there were about six vessels off hire and standing by for contracts, and two or three 'skeleton crews', who would maintain the vessels and, if and when the contracts came up, would jump onto the ship assigned for the job and just sail.

I think back, and I was checking on things; bearing in mind that you only had one or two hours' notice prior to sailing. I checked the fridges and freezers and they were empty, so I got hold of the operations manager and told him. He instructed my crew to board one of the other vessels from our company and take what we needed, which we did. It amazed me that they could keep track of the stores and/or equipment! Some of the food was past its sell-by date, but we had to go with what there was.

I was on the 'Gulf Fleet 36' and we had got a last-minute job sailing to an island in Indonesia to take equipment for preventing a blow-out. It was a small island, off Surabaya to the north. We went to the loading dock and I noticed that another of our company's vessels was loading at the same time and going to the same location. Strangely enough, the captain was the marine manager who was based in Brunei. When he saw me, he did not look impressed, but I walked away smiling to myself; full of contentment that he had been moved off from the shore job he had abused.

We got loaded up and sailed away to the island, which took about 36 hours steaming time. We offloaded at the small dock and also at the drilling rig, which was nearby, then off we went back to Singapore.

We arrived back in Loyang Base and, again, it was like musical boats! We just cleaned up the vessel, ready for the next job.

I was on standby, which was not good, as you never knew where you stood. You could be in your bed when you get called for a job, or just to move the ship, as someone needs to get out to go to the loading berth. It was ridiculous sometimes.

A few days later, we got another 'run job', so I said, "Yes, OK. No problem." Then they told me, "Oh! Not this ship; you have to move all your gear to the 'Chieftain Service'". This was not a bad ship; it had horsepower of around 8000 to 9000, so it was pretty reasonable for any work. So, I moved across and prepared for the next job.

We moved the ship to Loyang Base and started loading equipment for Total Oil, based in Thailand. We had to rendezvous with one of their ships, to do a sea transfer with fuel, and the deck cargo would be offloaded at the dock. The Total representative came on board with paperwork etc. Also, as we were carrying some cargo for another company, called Care Offshore, their representative was on board. The Care Offshore representative was a Chinese

Singaporean, and he was a nice fellow. He gave me his business card and said to contact him, and if he could help me, he would.

We set off for Thailand and completed the job with Total. I was instructed by my company to rendezvous with a heavy lift barge that needed towing back to Jurong Base in Singapore. We met with the heavy lift barge, which was owned by Nippon Steel, and had a meeting about the job. So, we picked the anchors up, connected our towing cable up and commenced towing back to Singapore. The weather conditions were good, so all seemed to be well.

The chief officer and I split the watches; we would do six hours on duty and then have six hours of rest, which was normal. I would be on watch from 6am to midday, then 6pm to midnight.

One time, for no specific reason, the tow wire had jumped over the rail and was caught between the ship's side and the hanging fender (tyre) which was supported by two chains. I thought that if I just increased the power, the wire would just cut through the chain. So I increased the power, but did it break the chain? No way. It just would not break.

Eventually, I decided to go dead slowly, so there was minimum weight resting. I got out acetylene and oxygen, leaned over and cut the chain. The wire was free again, and back to normal. It was not difficult; it was just annoying that it would not free itself! Anyhow, it all went well, so we settled back down to continue with the towing of the barge.

We were about two days away from Singapore and all was going fine. At midday, I was relieved by the chief officer and went down to my cabin. After a while, I was just dozing off, then I felt the ship vibrating badly and knew we were going astern. I immediately jumped out of bed and shot up to the bridge. As I was moving to the bridge, I was shouting to the chief officer, "Hit the emergency stop!" I think he was panicking, as he was all over the place.

I banged the stop down myself, but knew it was too late. Although I shut down the main engines, there was a lot of momentum, and the heavy lift barge collided with us.

When all had quietened down, I assured the people on the barge that all was fine, and after complete inspection of the stern and steering room, we could see that we had just put a gash in the stern roller at the top. It would not be a problem, if the weather stayed fine. I spoke again to the people on the barge and they were happy to continue.

So, once again, we got underway for Singapore. I knew this was not my trip, as a little bit later on, one of our main engines went down, which halved our power, but it was OK, as we were still managing a good speed, so I just carried on. I had a meeting with the officers on my ship, to determine the reason for the ship going astern. The chief engineer told me he was changing power from one generator to the other and, of course, the generator could not take the load and just blacked out the vessel. With this design of vessel, when there is a blackout, the engines automatically go into full astern. This design was reviewed later and subsequently altered.

I called my office in Loyang Base and told them of our position, and, to be safe, asked them to send us another tow vessel to take over the tow when approaching Jurong anchorage.

Our office replied, "Yes, no problem. We will send 'Jaramac 66'", which was a catamaran-design tow vessel only, but it was more than sufficient. I told them the time we would be passing Loyang, so that the other vessel could come out and take the tow, and I also told them when I expected to be at Jurong anchorage.

So the other vessel came and relieved me, only when I had already put the heavy lift barge in position at Jurong anchorage and he let his anchor drop and it was confirmed he was in a safe position. Then the other vessel arrived and the captain said, "Is there anything I can do?" I just ignored him and spoke to the barge captain, and he thanked me and everything, then I steamed away, back to Loyang Base for repair to the stern roller and further standby. By this time, I was getting a little bit fed up of how things were going, and no, I was not impressed by it one little bit.

We got back to the dock at Loyang Base and the company sent down welders and riggers to repair the damage, which was superficial. They had it repaired and painted very quickly. At this time, I went to the office and asked them if things were quiet on the spot market, and they said "Yes," so I asked about sending me home, as I had nearly done my time. They really looked down at me and I got some nasty remarks from administration, so I just said, "Forget it."

During the next couple of days, I decided to give this man a phone call (the one we took cargo for) and he invited me to his office. We had a brief meeting and he told me he was the local operations manager for Care Offshore, whose head office was in Switzerland. I gave him copies of my certificates to forward to the head office and see what materialises.

I thanked him and returned to my vessel at Loyang Base, pondering my future. By this time, I had been employed by Tidewater for about 12 years. Again, I went to the office and they said they were sending me home, as things were quiet. Yet when I had asked previously, they'd just snubbed me!

I got my flight ticket and told them I would not be back, as I had resigned. They just looked at me and said, "We have heard the same old story many times before," and I replied, "Not from me, you haven't!" They said, "You will be back," but I just kept quiet.

I arrived home and I think I was only home for about two weeks before Tidewater called and asked me to return, as they were starting to get busy. I told them, "Please remember what I told you before I left your office. I will not be returning." They were a bit upset but, again, to me, it did not mean anything.

So there I was, out of work!

They say the good Lord works in strange ways. . . a couple of days later, I got a phone call from Care Offshore, Switzerland, asking me if I would like to work for them. "Yes," I answered. I'd be going back to Singapore for Care Offshore, but making a diversion to Switzerland, to see the management.

I left home in December 1993 and headed for my new company. I was full of thoughts, regarding what the new company would be like and wondering about the agreements. Soon I would have answers to all my questions.

I arrived in Switzerland and there was a chap waiting to take me to the office, in a place called Bursinel. We drove through some nice countryside and if I'd said I was heading towards an oil field-related company in the middle of vineyards, no one would have believed me.

We passed through the entrance of a huge chateau. It was like an old mansion; it was a real nice property. I met with the necessary people and they were so nice to me, and then I met the operations manager who, of course, was French (just about all the people in the office were French-speaking). The operation manager, who was named Marc Remondiere, was a gentleman. We had certain discussions and he welcomed me to the company. The financial benefits were substantial.

'Red Falcon', Care Offshore.

When I had met everyone, I left the office and went back to the airport to travel to Singapore.

I arrived in Singapore around the 10th December 1993 and boarded the vessel 'Red Falcon' (all the fleet were named after birds). The 'Red Falcon' was a fine vessel, which had anchor recovery chain lockers converted into a big turbine area for driving the fire monitors. She was classed as an A1 firefighting/anchor-handling vessel and was lying at anchor in West Jurong anchorage, on standby.

I had a Filipino crew with a French chief officer and chief engineer. We were put on a contract to Thailand, to work with Total Oil and Exploration Company. There were also a number of other Care Offshore vessels in the area. I had a good experience on board, as the vessel was so reliable, even though she was a mature vessel.

I spent three months on board, then went home for six weeks, which was not too bad a rotation. In my time on board, we did some fighting with our fire monitors, especially at the Bongkot

Terminal, where gasses had been escaping. Our job was to keep at a safe distance and form a water cascade with our fire monitors, while people were evacuated.

I ended up being with the 'Red Falcon' for about seven months in total, then after my holidays, I would sometimes go to another location.

I stayed around Southeast Asia for several years and, in this period, I was on board the 'Red Petrel' ('Hoi Hai Hen', 'The Red Bird', in Chinese). We were engaged in operations with the Australian drilling rig 'Ocean Princess', Thailand.

'Red Petrel', Care Offshore.

I thought that the personnel on board the rig (management) were a little ignorant. One time, we were working the rig, offloading casings, and it took about seven days to offload us, as our decks were completely full. When we got back to the port, I got a visit from the Care Offshore port captain, who was a very nice chap. He told me there was a problem between the rig/client and Care Offshore.

He went on to say that, apparently, whilst I was alongside the rig, I had not communicated with the rig. This remark was totally unacceptable and I was very angry.

The port captain went on to say several other things, so I demanded to be taken to his office, so that I could call the company's operation manager and hear his feelings on the situation. At that moment in time, I was ready to call it a day and walk off the vessel!

I was shaking with anger when I was dialling the phone number, and when I got through to our operations manager (a French gentleman) I told him the story and how I felt about it. He listened to me and told me, "Captain, the client is our customer and the customer is always right." At this point, I was getting even angrier, then he told me, "Captain, please hear me out," and went on to say that he had travelled out to Kuala Lumpur to sort out contracts and, in his opinion, all the people at the meeting were rude. He was certainly not impressed with them. Then he told me, "Captain, you will go back on board your vessel and sail back to the rig and if, for any reason at all, you have justification for complaint, you will then put the vessel off hire and sail back to Singapore. The decision is yours."

I was gobsmacked. I hadn't expected that kind of answer. I felt good, as I had the company's backing, and I knew I would not abuse this.

I went back on board the ship, we loaded cargo for the rig again and sailed.

I arrived at the rig, still fuming about the way I had been treated. I was going to see who had falsely accused me of a lack of communication.

I sailed the vessel back to the rig and as soon as I had secured it, I got my chief officer to stay on the bridge and requested the 'personnel basket' (which could hold four people at a time) so that I could go into the rig. I then boarded the rig and talk about red faces! It was so embarrassing for them. Each supervisor I approached answered me with, "No, Captain, it was not me." It was then that I felt really sad for them. It was as if they had nothing better to do with their lives than try to complain about other people.

Anyhow, life goes on, and later I went back to my vessel and continued with business.

A few days later, the rig informed me that it was preparing to move to a new location. Of course, my vessel was involved in this operation. I did all my checks, had meetings with the crew and gave instructions for work and rest periods, as the anchor retrieval was very arduous.

We commenced the move and it was during the decking of one of the rig's anchors that the anchor fluke must have 'punctured' the plate at the stern of the vessel. In the offshore industry, anything is possible. At this time, we did not realise that the stern roller had been punctured, and so we carried on with the retrieval of anchors. Afterwards, I was connected to the rig with my vessel's towing wire, which was the system for towing the rigs from A to B.

The towage plan was agreed on and we set sail for the Bongkot Field in Thailand Gulf. Please remember; there were numerous hurricanes/typhoons near the Philippines, which then came across the South China seas where we were working! At this time, all looked good, so we set sail with the rig and our sister vessel was running free with us.

During the tow, we examined the steering flat where we thought we had punctured the stern roller with the anchor. To our utmost disbelief, we found that the watertight door to the steering compartment would not open and that the compartment was full of water, which had pressurised the door. Eventually, we released the water and opened the door, and the sight was a complete shock.

All the electrical and hydraulic components were absolutely sodden and, of course, dead! This meant that we could not use our karm fork on deck (used for releasing the rig at any given time). The chief engineer on the vessel, Joachim Treptow, really was magnificent. I truly respect him for his part in what followed.

To assess the situation, we had to pump out the steering room. We needed a semi-submersible pump and we did not have one on board, but luckily our sister ship did. By this time, the weather was getting worse and I was the master of the tow, so informed the rig of our situation. Naturally, they were concerned. I told them our plan.

Our sister vessel ('Red Plover') did, thankfully, pass over the pump to us. It was very tricky, with the weather conditions, and I was towing this massive semi-submersible rig behind me, so was restricted in my manoeuvrability.

We commenced pumping out the water in the steering area (thankfully, the steering system was still operable). Joachim estimated that it would take three days to fix. I knew he could repair it, but time was of the essence.

As we were towing along, we were getting weather forecasts, and I was making decisions about whether to abort the operation not.

A strong storm was coming. At that time, I informed the rig of my intention, which was, instead of going towards the Thailand Gulf, to turn around and head towards Singapore. This way, we would be essentially running away from the storm.

The rig was not too pleased with my decision, but my primary concern was for the safety of everyone on the rig and supporting vessels.

We did alter course and head down towards Singapore. The weather got worse, as expected, and of course we had constant communication with the rig. Our pumps were managing to keep the water at bay and the chief engineer was doing an excellent job of repairing the electronics and hydraulic system in the steering room.

I decided to keep towing away from the storm, which we were plotting on our navigation chart.

When the storm had eased off, I informed the rig of my intentions, turned the vessel around and headed back towards our intended location.

We got the rig back to its intended position and deployed the anchors, then we discharged some equipment belonging to the rig i.e. firefighting and oil dispersant chemicals.

The rig was giving me such a sob story. I just sailed away without so much as a by your leave and proceeded to Singapore to repair our stern roller. It only took a very short while to repair, then I departed for home, having been on board for over three months.

In the year of 1994, I was sent to China and joined the 'Red Swan'. To me, the vessel was perfect! She was an ex-Norwegian pipe carrier and had onboard positioning control with two main engines and two bow thrusters. The ship was a dream to handle. The accommodation was excellent too; I couldn't complain about anything. The crew on board were mainly Asian and very professional.

**Platform Supply Vessel, 'Red Swan',
with 'Maersk Supporter', offshore China.**

I joined the ship in a place called Shekouh Chiwan, which was very close to Hong Kong, and the client was a company called Arco. The platform we serviced was near an island to the south called Hainan, and it would take me about 48 hours of steaming to get there. Of course, we had to navigate the Hong Kong channel, which took about six hours, and the further 42 were spent on open seas.

When I arrived, it was just a large satellite platform with a drilling rig unit positioned on top, as well as the accommodation for the rig crew.

The rig company at that time was called Dual Drilling. The people on the rig were good to work with and yes, for me, it was good, steady work.

We were working with a Maersk vessel called 'Maersk Supporter' and the crew on board was also good people, as every Sunday, we would change out with the 'Maersk Supporter'; one would stay in the field for safety and the other vessel would return to port.

I had a really good cook from the Philippines and he would always prepare a typical English lunch i.e. roast beef and Yorkshire puddings. When the weather was good, our two vessels would secure to each other and the crew from 'Maersk Supporter' would come across and have a good lunch with us. In turn, I would get a lot of videos for my crew, so yes, life was good.

This job was going along OK, then, as my ship was so large, the port requested to use it as an offshore warehouse. Our deck would be full of containers and the people on the rig would need this equipment.

So off I sailed. On location was a mooring buoy, which we would secure to when we weren't needed.

When the rig called, I would go alongside it, then the people would come down in the Billy Pugh personnel basket and point out what they needed. They would return to the rig, then we would discharge the items. I must admit that the planning was

193

good, as we only had to visit the rig twice, maybe three times per day for short periods.

'Seabulk Puffin', formerly 'Red Puffin'.

In January 1995, I was assigned to the 'Red Puffin' in Singapore. She was on standby, waiting for work, and an ex-'Viking Supply', which was Norwegian, so she was a sturdy vessel. Again, I had a very good Philippine crew.

A contract came up. We had French owners, but brokers based in Singapore, and they would get the company contracts/work etc.

I had to steam to Malaysia, offshore, to meet up with a semi-submersible rig called 'Marine 500'. Of course, our job was to assist in mooring his anchors and then supply them.

We met up and, as he was under his own power, we just followed behind to Vietnam to set him up for the local company.

Everything was going well. I knew the barge master from years previously.

We would run into the port of Vungtau and replenish supplies etc. then return to the rig.

One time, we were working from Kemaman in Malaysia, but the rig was actually operating in Thai waters, so it was a joint contract between Malaysia and Thailand.

I remember one night, into the early morning, we had moved the rig and I had run all the rig's anchors out, as we were the only anchor-handling vessel. It was about 2am and I was sitting on the bridge in the dark, just relaxing. I had an AB (deckhand) on the bridge with me as lookout, but we were barely drifting in the general area, so all was good, including the sea conditions and visibility.

Then, from nowhere, we heard this slight whistling sound, which we thought was very unusual! So we were really listening and yes, we heard it again.

We went onto the wing of the bridge and it was pitch dark. The sound was getting louder! We then saw a man in the water with a lifejacket on, floating near us and blowing the whistle attached to the lifejacket.

I immediately sounded the general alarm and the crew came out on deck. I spoke to them over the public announcement system and told them what was happening.

A few minutes later, we had the survivor on board.

He seemed in good health, with no sign of any injuries, so we got him warm and gave him food and liquids. He managed to speak some broken English, and then he told us his story.

He had been on a Thai fishing boat, and it seems as if all the crew members were intoxicated. Then knives were brought out and everyone was fighting! This chap told us he had been afraid, so had grabbed the lifejacket and jumped into the sea! He believed he had been in the sea sometime, so he was ever so lucky that we rescued him, as there were no other vessels for miles! Had we not rescued him. . . well, I think he may have died. So yes, he was a very lucky man!

Of course, we told the rig what was happening, and our supply vessel was approaching, so the captain knew what was happening. The rig company representative was not too happy, as he said that they had to fly the man back to Malaysia via helicopter, and that it would be classed as illegal entry! But, to me, he was a distressed person and needed assistance to be repatriated.

Anyhow, after all the political conversations (our survivor didn't have any form of identification about his person), the helicopter took him away and I never heard anything about the incident again. I made a formal report and sent it to my company who, in turn, forwarded it on to the client and relevant parties

Like anything else, all things come to an end, and the time came (1996-7) to prepare to retrieve the rig's anchors. This was close to my time off, and my friend, Captain Philippe Monteville, would be coming on board to relieve me, so I was happy with that.

Prior to Philippe's arrival, we had already commenced anchor-handling operations for the 'Marine 500' to depart the area.

The weather seemed to be slowly getting worse. Anyhow, the helicopter arrived, Philippe came down and we started to do our handover, so that I could depart the vessel and go home. Philippe was telling me that the rig mover on board the rig was not a nice man, so it seemed that Philippe might be in for a bit of a tough time.

Anyhow, the handover was complete and I told Philippe that I would make arrangements to catch the helicopter from the rig.

I called up to the rig and asked about a helicopter flight to the shore. It seemed like the rig mover was refusing me leave of the vessel! I had never experienced this situation before. I asked to speak to the rig mover and he came on and said he was not letting me off the ship! His comments were duly noted in the ship's official log book.

So Philippe and I sat down and discussed the situation. We were the only anchor-handling vessel available. We agreed to contact our operation's manager in Switzerland and let him know the situation. He was very supportive.

We started, again, to retrieve the anchors. Company policy was that any damages had to be recorded and signed by the rig mover. We had sustained some slight damage to our deck boards, so documents needed to be signed.

The rig mover absolutely refused to sign. He was just being foolish. We called our operation's manager again and carefully explained the situation to him. He replied, "You are on board and I am not, but you have my full support." That was what we needed to hear.

Philippe and I decided to continue doing our jobs, but if we received more aggravation from the rig mover, we planned to stop and withdraw completely.

We recommended the anchor retrieval operation and, once again, the rig mover was very sarcastic towards us. For example, our vessel was called the 'Red Puffin' (all were named after seabirds) and he was saying things about us 'puffing along' and being 'just a smoky old tug', which upset Phillipe and myself a lot.

So, we decided so refuse the job and stop operations.

When we told the rig mover, he just laughed at us and continued with his sarcasm, which, again, irritated us.

Anyhow, we stopped operating but stayed in the general area, monitoring the situation.

The rig mover began to understand the reality of the situation and started begging us to re-join the operation. We declined. Then he managed to gather up the courage to say that he did not need us.

He called a local anchor-handling vessel from Vungtau, which was run by a British captain (the rig mover's friend, it turned out to be).

The local vessel came out and the rig mover was chatting on the VHF with his 'friend', giving him instructions to retrieve a certain anchor. and of he went and called back and said, "yes, all OK, now chasing out to the anchor" etc. The work got underway but it was clear that the master of the vessel just could not do the job. The rig mover started asking us to forgive him and apologised for the verbal abuse he had given us and so on.

Eventually, the vessel master got the job completed, but it was a complete joke! The 'Marine 500' and its British rig mover retrieved the anchors and went off into the horizon.

We went into Vungtau and I signed off and departed the vessel.

When I arrived in Vungtau, I had to fly down to Jakarta, and then on to a place called Balikpapan, Indonesia, to relieve the master on board 'Red Penguin'. I had never been to this place, so it was interesting to see what the culture was like.

I arrived in Jakarta and was waiting for my connection to Balikpapan. I was sitting in the lounge, along with the other passengers, of which there were not too many.

I kept asking people, "Why the delay?" and "How much longer will we be waiting?" and they would say, "Not too long now!"

I had instructions from my office to withdraw 1000 US dollars from the funds (which had, of course, been agreed by the incoming master). So there I was, delayed in Jakarta, with 1000 US dollars; the cash advance the crew were looking forward to receiving.

We, the passengers, were getting fed up with waiting and walking up and down, with no information and no food. It was getting a bit silly! Some of the passengers had children with them, and they needed to eat. Then, one of the passengers happened to look at the television and told me to come and look.

When I saw the TV, I was shocked. It was the local news, and it showed rioting going on in the streets! People were running amok, throwing fire bombs and setting fire to cars and properties. It looked like a war zone! To say the least, I was concerned.

We found out that the airport was on lockdown; nobody out and nobody in, especially the section we were in.

The airline company was called Garuda Airways which, I think, was government-run. They told us that they could not get us into airport hotels; due to the riots, all the hotels were fully occupied. They also said that they could not take us to hotels outside of the airport, as they could not guarantee our safety. So, really, we were prisoners in the airport! There were plenty of security people around, so that made us feel somewhat safer.

We were told that this could go on for a further two days, and to get our baggage. I made a bed out of my clothes, so that I could at least lie down.

The company representative obtained food boxes and soft drinks for us, but I was beginning to feel a little bit nervous about the situation.

This went on for about 36 hours. It seemed as if there was a revolt between the local Indonesian people and the Chinese.

Finally, on the TV, we saw policemen and soldiers calming everything down.

So eventually, the rioting stopped and the flights resumed. I departed for Balikpapan, which was only about an hour's flight away.

On my arrival, I was met by our company's agent, who drove me to the hotel. I knew I would have to stay there for a day or so. I got a good night's rest and tried to forget about what had just happened.

The next day, I had to change the 1000 US dollars for the crew's cash advances, so I went with the agent to the bank. Normally, the rate was one US dollar equals about three rupiah (I think that was the currency!) Anyhow, due to the riots etc. all the currencies fell, and one US dollar was worth 17 rupiah! So you can imagine how many notes I had on me!

I hurried back to the hotel and asked them to place the money in the hotel safe, but they smiled and said it wouldn't fit in! Consequently, I had to put it in my case and lock it! I then stayed in my hotel room, waiting for the agent to give me information.

The agent rang me and said that we would be boarding a small boat to take me to my vessel, 'Red Penguin', which was working not too far offshore.

So, we boarded the small boat at the port of Balikpapan and, as we were sailing, I looked around. It seemed a big port, with deep water, so I thought that manoeuvring my vessel alongside wouldn't be a problem. I would follow up with sea charts and harbour charts etc. once on board.

I boarded the vessel about 30 minutes later and all was fine. I did a good handover with the outgoing master, who was a German chap. The chief officer and the chief engineer were also German and seemed decent chaps.

After the handover was completed and I had told the crew of the events in Jakarta, then issued them with their cash advances, the outgoing master disembarked.

I got settled down to see what the job entailed and had meetings with the crew, so all was going well.

We were close to shore, working for Total, and the rig was a jack-up called 'Rani Woro'. All was fine. Then the time came for me to take the vessel to port for more supplies etc.

Of course, I thought I would be entering the main port or at least a large port in Balikpapan, but that was not to be.

The mate was a local chap, which was good for me, as he had lots of local knowledge and he helped me in proceeding to the supply base.

We entered this very narrow, buoyed channel, and there we picked up a local pilot, before travelling up the jungle rivers.

I had never experienced anything like this! For example, we had to keep close to the islands, as the water was at its deepest there. We were so close that the overhanging branches from the trees were sweeping along the ship's side, and we could actually see monkeys and orangutans in the trees! For me, this was spectacular.

We continued the navigation around islands and bends in the river, and then we got the full flow of the current, and yes, it was strong!

The oil company we were working for, Total, did have some kind of loading dock, but the problem was that my vessel was too big and deep to enter! So, we dropped our anchor midstream, and when all was settled down, all the cargo and materials were delivered by barges with small tugs pulling them. This was a real eye-opener!

One of the problems we experienced was that my vessel was out of trim. For example, we would need lots of fuel to ballast the ship down and were told that there was a shortage of fuel. So we only got half of what we needed. Then, for the deck cargo, we would get completely full of drill pipes etc, on the stern, so at the end of the loading and offloading operation, we would then try to get the ship back onto an even keel, and sometimes we didn't have the tanks for moving the ballast around. So at certain times, we would depart the anchorage with the vessel being deeper at the stern than at the bow.

I remember the first time it happened. We departed the anchorage for the rig, and we had a pilot on board, which was compulsory. Ahead of us were other vessels, so basically, we would follow the leader. As you were moving along, you might find that the vessel in front of you had stopped. Of course, it had run aground!

When this happened, my pilot instructed me to go around the grounded vessel and carry on up the channel as normal. There was never any damage to the vessels, as the riverbed was sheer mud, so the grounded vessels would just wait for the next high tide and be free to continue on their journey. It was amazing how it worked!

I remember one time, we were secured to the rig and transferring materials, liquids etc. and I was sitting on the bridge, just observing things. Then, out of the rig's drilling tower, came a gush of cement-like chemical, and I realised that, while they were drilling, they'd had a kick, which just sends everything to the surface and, if not controlled quickly, would lead to a blow-out. This is absolutely not what you want.

I spoke to the rig's barge engineer via radio. Up to then, he had no idea what was happening. Straight away he did the business, and I released all the hoses and moorings and picked up my anchor to stand by, in case the rig had to be evacuated.

I went back alongside and that is when they were putting all non-essential personnel into lifeboats to lower them to sea. They would come alongside me and we would take the people and keep them safe on our ship.

It took quite a while to get the rig under control, after the kick they had experienced.

When I received the call, I moved back into the rig and discharged the rig people, as the rig had sent down the 'personnel basket'.

When everyone was back on board, the barge engineer instructed me to return to the rig and continue with the operation. I declined and told him that I was in charge of my vessel and crew and deemed the situation a little bit too dangerous at that point. He agreed, and about 12 hours later, I decided to start up operations. After that, the rest of the rig visit went smoothly and safely, which all parties appreciated.

I did a few runs to the rig, in and out the jungle river, then, after six weeks, my time was up, so I signed off the ship's articles and disembarked

'Red Fulmar', formerly 'HMS Red Fawn',
from the British Hydrographic Sector.

In September 1995, I was sent to Abidjan on the Ivory Coast. The local language was French, which I had no command of whatsoever, but I got by!

I was assigned to a seismic survey vessel ('Red Fulmar') which was moored up alongside at Carina shipyard.

When I stepped on board, it was completely different from your anchor-handling vessel; not dissimilar to a yacht. It was painted in white (the hull, that is) and the decks were made of wood. It had been well-maintained; the decks were in immaculate condition. It was an ex-HMS vessel ('HMS Fawn') and had been bought by Care Offshore and named 'Red Fulmar'.

You can imagine the space, as it was fitted out to carry 50 ratings, plus the officers. It was a 'proper' ship!

We did a couple of trips with the survey crew, then on the way back to port, we had an engine problem. When we got moored up, the chief engineer informed me of the situation, and it was a big job.

The chief engineer and I informed the office of the situation and the chief engineer ordered the spares etc. We waited six weeks for delivery, then we found out that the chief had ordered the wrong parts, which caused extra delay. This was too much, plus, in this shipyard, there was quite a lot of disturbance, with locals trying to take things from the vessels.

Next to us came a Korean fishing trawler and, of course, the crew would be drinking etc. One time, in the night, it seemed that a local canoe had come alongside and two locals boarded the Korean vessel. They did not know that the Korean crew had a German Shepherd and, of course, the dog was let loose, attacked the locals and broke their canoe! They were thrown into the dock and that was that!

The next morning, the local police showed up and the Korean captain was telling me, "No problem, no problem," and, of course, he was correct. He did some haggling with the local police, a few bottles of alcohol exchanged hands, and all went away merrily! There were also coups, where the public took to the streets demonstrating, guns were fired etc. We were safe, as in the dockyard, the gates were locked, and security were on high alert.

This is how it was in Abidjan, but the French troops would be around to keep the peace.

I remember staying there for a while, then we towed the rig, 'Ocean Liberator', away to Ghana, but on the odd occasion I would return to Abidjan for supplies.

On 21st January 1995 I was sent to Zhanjiang, China, to be captain of 'Red Petrel'. It was strange, as very few of the people I was working with spoke English. I hoped things would get easier.

The client would come down to the jetty to see us, each time we arrived and departed, and yes, he was very involved with us. The only problem was that he could not speak English, so we hired a Chinese English-speaking third officer to translate, which was fine.

The funny thing was that the client, who was elderly, would always come to see us dressed in a suit and tie, yet wore a large pair of wellington boots with it, due to the environment around the dockside.

The chief officer was Phillipe (a Frenchman, of course) and we had sailed together previously. He was a trustworthy chap, so all was good there.

The client came down to the ship and kindly asked me if I would mind sailing back to the rig to let the Chinese vessels back into port to celebrate the Chinese New Year. Of course, that wasn't a problem.

We departed Zhanjiang and headed towards the channel, which was a very long one. The Chinese Navy base was next to the supply base, so we had the Navy has friends. The navigation route was not the best and you had to be ever so careful, as there were numerous buoys around, which made navigation dangerous. The client would always call me to check that we had passed the 'dangerous' points (the buoys) no matter what time of day.

We arrived at the rig and offloaded our equipment. We were then on standby, in case of any emergencies.

When we were up close to the rig, I would see about twenty Chinese people standing outside the radio room, looking around, as if something were about to happen. To me, it looked strange!

One day, there was a small fishing boat and the rig told me to go and investigate. So, off I went, and I got the third mate to speak to the captain of the small boat. It was a Vietnamese fishing boat which had got its nets caught in the propeller, and the captain was trying to clear the net.

The third mate passed this information to the rig, and it sounded as if the rig people were very nervous and wanted to get the boat away as quickly as possible, which did not seem correct, as the fishing boat was disabled.

The fishing boat did eventually get clear and move away. I think it was all about politics, with the Chinese bordering the Vietnamese. Maybe the rig was slightly on the Vietnamese side as opposed to the Chinese side. As they say, stranger things happen at sea!

I got back into the standby routine as the weather became bad. It was about force 8 on the Beaufort Wind Scale, so it was uncomfortable. The wind was just pounding the ship, which was moving at slow speed into the oncoming seas. Plus, it was February and still cold.

I was sitting on the bridge and the Navtex machine started to sound an alarm. There was a vessel sinking, with 15 crew on board. I checked the position and he was relatively close to us. I knew it was highly unlikely that the rig would release us to investigate. Regardless, I spoke to the third mate and explained the situation. He, in turn, relayed the information to the rig who, surprisingly, said, "Yes, go ahead." With nothing else to say, I proceeded to the vessel in distress.

On our arrival, there was still no change in the wind or sea condition, and I was very close to the sinking vessel. It was a small cargo vessel and there were lots of boxes floating around. At this time, the vessels decks were just submerging, so it looked pretty grim.

I saw the distressed crew with their lifejackets donned, but none of them were abandoning the ship! To me, they seemed too afraid to jump into the sea, so that I could pick them up.

I waited a while to assess the situation, and the only way I could receive the distressed seamen was by manoeuvring my ship and slightly touching their vessel, so that they could jump ship to ship. I know this was asking for a great deal of skill and luck, but I thought that if I didn't do it, there would be no survivors.

So I briefed my crew on my intentions. The weather was still bad, but I had my crew with me, at least for a couple of months. They were Filipinos and a good crew.

I nudged the stricken ship for the first time, and I believe about three members of the crew jumped across. Then we got pushed away by the weather. I regrouped and went in for another try; receiving five or so more. This I kept doing until everyone had been accounted for, unharmed.

I felt pretty pleased with myself and proud of my crew, whom ushered the survivors into the accommodation. They were given showers, dry clothing, food and liquids. I then proceeded to port. I kept close to the area and watched the vessel sink gradually out of sight, then altered course to take the people to safety. All through this operation, my third mate had been the communications man, and he was constantly in touch with the Chinese Navy.

About two hours later, the master of the vessel came up to the bridge. He so humble; he could not thank me enough. His crew came up, one by one, to thank me and the crew for our brave actions, and I was pleased that all was good. The master explained to me that the crew had been afraid to jump into the sea, even though they had lifejackets on. I think I would have felt the same, but I never told them that!

As we continued to move away from the sunken vessel, the Chinese Navy approached and gave me instructions to follow them, which I did, and I entered the mouth of an estuary, where a naval vessel came alongside and picked up all the survivors. Then I returned to the drilling rig, to stand by, awaiting further instructions. As far as I was concerned, that was that!

We were on standby at the rig for a few days more, and the weather was not good, to say the least!

Well, the Chinese New Year was over, so I was relieved by one of the Chinese vessels and returned to Zhanjiang port. As we approached the dockside, I had never seen so many people or cameras! I told the chief mate that there may be some high-ranking people around.

I was manoeuvring the vessel close to the dock, and all the people with cameras had red ribbons and things, and they were all pointing at us! I felt a bit on edge!

Once the vessel was secured and our gangway out, the people came rushing on board! Then it came to me. . . news of our rescue had got back to town!

The owner of the sunken vessel and the rescued crew were the first on board and, of course, we told the owner what had happened. The local television were broadcasting my talk with the owner!

All the people (and there were many) applauded us, and it was a bit overwhelming for me, as I just felt that I had done my best, and that we had been in the right place at the right time.

The local Lord Mayor came on board and congratulated us all. He was very thankful to us for rescuing his people. They declared the town open to our ship and my crew members were very happy, as they were of Asian origin. All in all, it was satisfying! As they say; job done!

After that day, myself and my crew were well-respected and, for sure, it left me feeling very good!

In October 1998, I was on a small but powerful tug called the 'Red Eagle II' and was sent to Brunei. I relieved the outgoing master and we were support for a heavy lift construction crane barge.

The people were good and the job would soon be coming to an end. We towed the heavy lift barge back to Singapore and said our farewells, then I put the barge on standby at West Jurong anchorage and departed. I went alongside, as we had minor repairs to do. We needed our sharks jaw (a machine for securing wires) to enable us to continue with our anchor-handling operations, and at the end of the previous contract, the sharks jaw went out of action, so yes, it was imperative for us to get it repaired.

So we commenced on some maintenance work, then, a short while later, we got another contract with the same heavy lift barge. That suited me very well, as I knew who we would be working with. The barge would be sailing on its own power, and we would catch up. This time the destination was Gulf of Kutch, India!

We arrived and, of course, we had to go through the country's formalities. I must admit, it was not too impressive, the way this was conducted. We commenced our operations and things were going well. We would move the anchors around for the heavy lift barge, so that he could position himself in good, safe-lifting mode.

A few years previously, there had been a hurricane and the offshore terminal was completed destroyed; hence all the units were in the process of being rebuilt. The terminal went onto the shore, and where it reached shore, small draught vessels were able to secure to a small wooden jetty. There was nothing else; no commercial vessels could approach, due to the shallow draught limitations.

This is why all the materials etc. were brought in on dumb barges from the Persian Gulf states. So, as you will appreciate, we could work safely at the seaward end of the terminal but were unable to go further in.

When our construction barge was operating at the seaward end of the terminal, it was great for me, as I could manoeuvre the vessel anywhere without worrying about grounding, plus we had to do a lot of anchor-running at tide times i.e. when the tide was rising, giving me more water depth in which to move the vessel safely. Everything was fine. I did the anchor-running myself but got a decent rest once we had put the heavy lift barge on location.

Then, as time went by, so the heavy lift vessel moved closer to the shore, at which point things started to get a bit tricky, to say the least! I would back my ship up close to the heavy lift vessel, whose crane would then pass me his anchor down, and connect to his wire, and then I would steam out to a drop position. However, I was also getting instructions from the surveyor, who was based on the heavy lift vessel.

We could only run this anchor at high water, and it was high water now, at midnight. I had previously received the charts from the heavy lift vessel surveyor, and the course and distance, plus the water depth, all looked good. So there I was, about to run this anchor and, as I explained, the terminal was being rebuilt, so it was pretty hectic, with boats etc. all moving around.

I started to move off towards the given position. I had my forward searchlight on, pointing in the direction I would be going. Then, from nowhere, there was the seabed; just absolutely shallow water, and when I say shallow, I mean shallow! I stopped the engines immediately and started going back towards the heavy lift vessel on the reciprocal course. I called the heavy lift vessel and started to complain, stating that the work scope here was very dangerous and would be impossible to be complete.

Everyone was confused, saying things like, "No, that's impossible, it cannot be" etc. I told them they were welcome to come on board and see for themselves, but I knew they would not come.

Eventually, it was accepted that the area was not good enough to anchor up the heavy lift vessel. The best plan of action would be to skip that project for the time being and maybe return if they found a solution. I told them the depth of water where the anchor should be placed. There would be no fish (but maybe rabbits!) All I saw was mud and green weed, and I was amazed that anyone could overlook this.

Anyhow, on with the project! The heavy lift vessel required materials very often, so the smaller tugs would bring barges from Dubai, filled with the necessary materials. When they got close, it was my job either to assist the tugs to come alongside the heavy lift vessel, or even take the barge from the tugs. Then, I would have to position it alongside the heavy lift vessel, and it was a struggle, as sometimes the current strength was up to 5 knots, with no lighted buoys and small spaces to manoeuvre in.

It was becoming a nightmare, and I thought, "Surely they cannot give me any other work to do, as I am getting quite stressed!" I got a call from the heavy lift vessel (in the past, I did go on the vessel and talk to the people, and they seemed OK). I was told to go outside the channel and assist their other barge! I thought, "Is there no end to this torture?"

So, I moved outside and saw the barge. I had to replace a tug with a problem. My job was to continuously run anchors as he was laying pipe line. So he was moving ahead, and I was running the anchors non-stop. I was not too impressed, as with this kind of work, you need two boat handlers and my chief mate was not confident enough to help me. However, it would only be for a couple of days, so I thought I could manage it.

Some of the instructions given to me were just ridiculous. For example, I had to back up very close to the barge to wait for the crane to lower down the anchor, and the barge's chief mate would instruct me to hold position. This was OK for a few moments, but I had all sorts of environmental forces pushing me, so it was impossible to stay there for long. This chief mate was getting angry, and the language was not nice. I informed the chief mate that he did not need an anchor-handling tug, but a motor car with the brake applied! Of course, he was not too pleased with my reply. Sometimes, the radio conversations were so extreme than the barge's captain got involved.

It was like this for some time, until I accomplished my mission and returned to the heavy lift barge. The strange thing about this incident was that, a few years down the line, I was working in Nigeria (not through choice) and had some cargo for a Saipem rig (an Italian company). So I called in on my approach and explained what my work scope was. A voice came on and said, "Captain! How are you, my friend? It's been a long time!" It was the barge's chief mate, who had been promoted! I just smiled to myself and spoke nicely to him this time.

I signed off the 'Seabulk Eagle II' in India and had my days off.

Later on, I was in Singapore, which was our base for Asia, when the technical superintendent asked me if I would go with him to the 'Seabulk Eagle II' to check how things were. Of course, I was not on contract and my ship was just laid alongside, so I agreed.

When we arrived on board, we were met by the captain, who told us about the problems with the ship. Straight away, I thought,

"This is strange," as when I was on board in India, we never had any out of the ordinary problems. I listened with interest and it turns out that the vessel propellers had been damaged through grounding etc. of which he had known nothing. Then he showed us the ship's official log book and said, "Oh look; here is a statement of the damage." The superintendent said that if it was logged, the office could claim on insurance.

So I looked at this statement and what I saw I had never seen before. The date of the report was one of the dates I had been in command of the vessel. Someone had forged my signature! When I saw this, I just went berserk. I asked the Captain, "Do you know who I am?" Of course, he said "No!" Then I told him, "I am the person whose signature you have forged!" He said it wasn't him etc. I was livid and the superintendent was trying to calm me down. I had to leave the ship to cool off. Needless to say, the captain received instant dismissal. I never heard what happened to him, but I certainly complained to our office!

His actions were completely unprofessional and totally disgusting.

I was moved about within the company, in keeping with their policy, and this was good for me, as I never got complacent.

While I was employed with Care Offshore, the good thing was that they rotated you around their vessels, so you went to different places on different types of vessel.

In October 1999, I was deployed to Buenos Aires to sail the tug/supply vessel 'Red Toucan', which was of Italian registry, but I was deemed fine to be in command of it.

I arrived in Buenos Aires and, please remember, feelings between Argentina and UK were not the best, due to the Falkland War in 1982.

'Red Toucan', 'Cadimare'.

I arrived and was met at the airport by the local agent, who took me straight to the vessel. I had been travelling a long time, so I had a word with the chief officer and chief engineer, then went to bed for a good sleep.

I woke up the next morning and, feeling very good, set about my quest to discover my work objectives. I was to tow a cargo vessel from Buenos Aires to Pakistan for scrap. At present, it was owned by a Greek company. By this time, the crew members were arriving. While the vessel was in Buenos Aires, there had just been a skeleton crew on board, but now we were beginning to fill up to normal crew level.

I had worked with the 'Red Toucan' previously, but never in command. The chief officer, chief engineer and I did our rounds, as it would be a good while before we got to Cape Town, South Africa, so we wanted to make doubly sure that all was running well in all departments.

I then decided to have a look at the vessel we were expected to tow to Pakistan for scrap.

I boarded the vessel and met the master (a Greek chap) who gave me a brief history of the vessel. He seemed a decent man. During the days of preparing the tow etc. he gave my crew lots of video tapes and bonded store cigarettes, so that was good of him!

I went to the bow of the vessel to see the rig-up of the towing wire, shock wire etc. and standard towing equipment, which was normal procedure.

I noticed that there was a very long emergency wire which was only 32mm in diameter. Under the circumstances, this was not very comforting, as the South Atlantic could be a very difficult and dangerous ocean to cross. Expected weather conditions were never too good, due to long swell periods coming in.

Anyhow, on with the job. We got everything secure, seaworthy and ready to sail. I remember that we had some shoreside people coming on board to check things too; certificates of trading etc. When they heard me talking English, I felt that they seemed to become more hostile. The only thing I could do was to transform their visit from an official one to a social one! I started talking about rugby, which they responded to immediately, and they seemed to forget all about politics and the Falklands!

Two pilots came on board and we kept the towed vessel on a short tow wire, as we were navigating the River Plate outward-bound, which took us quite some time, as we were only allowed to do a tow speed of around 3 knots or so.

The pilots disembarked at their station, and so we were bound for Pakistan via Cape Town, for fuel and stores etc. Once we were clear of small boats etc., we lengthened the tow to 800 metres, which would be a good length, and had a shock wire inserted, which would take the shock pull on the wire in high seas. Normally, if conditions were favourable, we would steer a course around the west, so that was my intention.

Initially, all was good. I set sail for the port of Cape Town, West Africa. Once we were beginning to lose the headland of Argentina, the swell started to increase and I decided to alter course, for a safer, slower and hopefully more comfortable journey. (How wrong I was!) The course I ended up on was a north-easterly one, which kept us in the swells, and we were rocking and rolling!

The wind was increasing steadily, thereby energising the sea, and to say it was uncomfortable would be an understatement! No one on board slept well and we were in the middle of the south Atlantic with nowhere to run. There was absolutely nothing I could do, other than keep the vessel and our tow moving at minimum speed, so as not to cause any damage. Believe me, the passage was horrendous.

We were up and down for days and days, and all the crew members were unwell, due to the vessel motions. There were very few vessels around us, or even on radar, and the weather didn't seem to be letting up.

Then, one morning, the unexpected happened. The bad weather and force 10 wind broke the towing wire. There was not a thing we could do, except stay close to the cargo vessel, which was unmanned. So, for safety's sake, I had to make all the vessels in the vicinity aware of a crewless cargo vessel drifting around. I also broadcast on channel 16 (the call/emergency frequency).

I would say the swell was around 10 metres and the wind was constant; spraying the vessel all the time. I stayed in the vicinity of the vessel for a total of eight days, and then the weather started to ease off. In the middle of the South Atlantic, you always experience large swells, so we monitored the weather constantly and when the swell reduced to about five metres, I decided to go alongside the 'dead' vessel and attempt to reconnect the new tow wire to her. I held a meeting with all the crew and we had a detailed plan of what was going to happen.

I manoeuvred the vessel alongside and the chief mate and two seamen got on board. and I put the vessel in a good position and yes, we connected our new tow wire to the cargo vessel's emergency tow wire. I then picked up the crew and away we went, to lengthen the tow wire and hopefully resume service.

All went well and yes, we managed to get about 1200 metres of tow wire in between both vessels to make it safer and more comfortable. The weather was easing off, so I put us back on our original route, so that we were going to Cape Town directly. That felt really good; especially knowing that the crew could get back to normal i.e. eat well, carry out small inside maintenance work and also get a good rest.

Everyone was feeling good on board, and when I reset the course and checked positions, I discovered that the storm and currents had moved us slightly closer to Cape Town, which was better than nothing. So, we were on course, with a cargo vessel in tow, and all seemed good on board. Of course, during the bad weather, I had been in touch with all the company's people, as well as the client, informing them of our situation.

Like I said, we were all shipshape again and underway. When we got closer to Cape Town, I received information from our head office that we would be handing over the tow to one of our sister ships, as we were going to get a new contract with Maersk, out of Cape Town. So, my priority was to pass the tow over, then I would steam full speed to the dockyard to get some engine work done, so that we would be in good shape for the new contract.

Our sister vessel turned up when we were about 100 miles from Cape Town. I knew the captain; Phillipe Monteville, who was a good chap. The vessel was the 'Red Falcon', which I had commanded previously in Luanda. Phillipe had been telling me via email that he was joining us from Nigeria and had no fuel, water or food on board, so was in a desperate way.

The first thing we did when he arrived was supply him with fuel, water and food stores, as we had a good stock of each. The weather was not bad, but still a long way from being good. We carried out this operation, then carefully passed him the tow across, so that he was connected.

I gave him all the relevant information and then we set off, full speed, for Cape Town.

On arrival, we were met by our company's marine superintendent, who updated me on our job scope, repairs etc.

So, there we were in the dock, and I was kind of licking my wounds and getting everything ready for the next job.

A few days later, I received a call from our head office in Switzerland. The 'Red Falcon' would be approaching Cape Town soon and had engine problems. They had arranged for a Russian anchor-handling vessel to relieve the 'Red Falcon', take the tow and it safely offshore, which would enable the 'Red Falcon' to come into the dock for repairs. The office requested that I go on board the Russian vessel as a company rep for assisting the crew etc.

I boarded the Russian tug/supply vessel (I cannot remember the name) and we left the port and just stayed close to Simon's Town, to meet with 'Red Falcon'. I explained my expectations to the Russian master and he said, "Fine, yah!"

The 'Red Falcon' came close and I was telling the Russian master what was needed and he said, "No more, no more! You have maximum power!" (The ship was a good size). Finally, we aborted the mission as the Russian vessel was useless. I asked the Russian master to get close to the 'Red Falcon' so that I could jump across, and then the Russian vessel was released from duties.

When I got on board the 'Red Falcon', I went to the bridge to speak to the captain (my friend Phillipe) and we decided to go into Cape Town with the cargo ship in tow. A lot of work and permissions had been given prior to the port authorities, so that would save us time.

We explained the situation to the pilot and initially he was calm, so we proceeded to the harbour entrance. Just as we were about to go inside, the pilot started screaming, "Abort! Abort!" which, of course, was absolutely impossible. He was really screaming! This was because the wind had suddenly increased and was just gushing down Table Mountain.

There was absolutely nothing we could do.

By the skin of our teeth, we managed to get the 'convoy' inside. What a bloody relief that was for me, as this cargo vessel had been a nightmare ever since I boarded it in Buenos Aires!

We got the vessels swung around (remember that the 'Red Falcon' was one engine down and had a dead ship in tow!) Anyhow, with the pilot more relaxed now, we got the vessels securely to the dockside.

After a while, I told Phillipe I was going back to my vessel, which was just around the corner. I knew he was being relieved that evening and heading home to France, so I told him I would come back to the 'Red Falcon' to say cheerio to him, and away I went to see how life was on board the 'Red Toucan'. All was going well and I had my evening meal on board. I told my chief officer where I was going and went back to the 'Red Falcon'. To my surprise, there was man sitting on a dockside bollard, looking dejected. I said, "Good evening. Are you going on board the vessel?" and he replied that the master of the vessel had banned him! I kindly asked him his business, and he told me he was the owner of the vessel we had been towing across from Buenos Aires. So I was surprised, and I thought, "What kind of a man is the new master?"

I went on board. The master was a Frenchman who had relieved me earlier on one of our company vessels. I briefly spoke to him and wished him a safe trip, then I left his vessel, as I knew he would be preparing for departure.

I returned to my vessel and all went quiet.

Early in the morning, I had our company technical superintendent on board and we heard a story. A local fishing vessel had been sailing back into the port when it collided with a wall. The vessel had been towed out the previous night by the 'Red Falcon', but the crew had forgotten to get the lights running and, of course, it was pitch black; hence the collision!

In Cape Town, we got the 'Red Toucan' engines inspected and went onto a small contract, servicing a semi-submersible rig anchored up in Simon's Town. This was a good job and lasted about one week. Again, we were at the dock, just waiting for something to happen, and as the saying goes, "Wait and something will always come along."

I was in my bed, enjoying a good rest, free of any runs to rigs etc. when the telephone rang. It was the office in Switzerland. There was a vessel listing badly, with a cargo of timber, which needed help immediately. It was located about 120 miles north of Cape Town.

I started the main engines as the crew got the towing equipment ready and we set sail to look for the stricken vessel. The weather was not too bad, but along the coast, there was always a swell running.

When we arrived, there were a couple of smaller vessels around, in case the crew on the stricken vessel had to abandon. I got on the VHF radio and spoke to the master, who explained the situation to me. I was to approach and pass over my towing wire for the vessel to connect to, then we could tow it to safety.

The vessel was certainly listing badly, but it was stable, so we passed the tow wire across and the vessel's crew connected. I manoeuvred my vessel, took strain on the tow wire and did the necessary things to commence towing.

We started towing the vessel back to Cape Town, at a good speed of 6 knots, regularly conversing with the vessel's master to make sure all was OK on board. I intended to reach port at daylight, so that we could see everything clearly on approach.

It took 24 hours to get the vessel close to Cape Town, and I called the pilot and port authorities to explain the situation. The pilots would not give me permission to enter, as there was a strong wind blowing down from Table Mountain which, in turn, came directly across the harbour entrance.

My shore support team was also aware of the situation and started to make arrangements for me to go another port.

I turned the vessel around and started to head back north, to a place called Saldannah, which was a port for offloading iron ore and other deep draughted vessels. This was not a problem, as I knew the harbour had plenty of space to turn the vessels around if need be. I contacted the pilot station and all local authorities to inform them of my intentions, so all were on standby.

When I passed through the entrance, harbour tugs came alongside and I passed the disabled vessel to them. They secured the vessel alongside the dock. When we had got everything clear, I proceeded to go alongside and moor my vessel ahead of the disabled timber vessel.

Purely out of curiosity, I went on board the timber vessel. The deck load had moved to one side, causing the list. I found out that the cargo was freshly-cut trees from Africa, and I could see lizard-type creatures moving in and out of the cargo. The crew told me that the creatures would come out and attempt to bite the crew. That was enough for me! I immediately got back onto the dockside, passed all the relevant documentation to the vessel's master, had it signed and returned to me, then was on my way back to my vessel again.

We prepared the vessel for sailing and received clearance to depart Saldannah Port and head back to Cape Town, where I moored the vessel alongside and awaited new instructions.

At this time, our company, Care Offshore, was being taken over by an American company, so things were looking bleak.

I did one more trip from Southeast Asia, working for Harrods Oil which, in turn, belonged to Mohamed El Fayed, whose son was killed with Princess Diana in the tragic accident.

I stayed there until the company found a suitable relief for me, then I came home.

I had been at home a while and had reached a crossroads in my career. Which way should I move?

During my days in Egypt, while I was having my days off, I would go offshore in the capacity of MWS (Marine Warrant Surveyor), working on rig moves on behalf of the underwriter. I would fit in one or two moves, then return home to prepare for going back to the vessel.

Around February 2000, I was on board the vessel 'Red Swan' (once more) working from Pointe-Noire in West Africa. All of a sudden, I received a call from my company, instructing me to proceed to Nigeria to relieve one of our other vessels. I shared my thoughts and spoke out about this situation. I was definitely not in favour of this move. I had never been to Nigeria, but I had heard stories.

I voiced my concerns to my operations manager, but I had to go, and this would close the book once and for all.

We arrive in Nigeria and, on the way, I had communicated with the vessel we would be changing out with. It sounded as if we were going to war, not to be a supply vessel to oil rigs! The captain told me that they had been boarded by armed pirates, who had thrown a couple of the ship's crew into the sea and beaten others up!

The vessel was also carrying four armed Nigerian naval personnel to deter pirates. There had been skirmishes; two pirates had been shot dead on the deck of the supply vessel. The master had been instructed to return to port.

So, me being me, I was really taken aback and worried about what I was going into.

We arrived in Port Harcourt, Nigeria, and people just swarmed on board. It was not something I had previously experienced. We cleared the vessel and made preparations for the ship to be loaded and away we sailed to the drilling rig offshore.

On board, we had four military people who were loaded with weapons. An uneasy feeling came over me. The military would arrange themselves on the bridge with me. They set out their weapons and equipment in case of any 'attacks'.

We arrived at the rig and all seemed nice and tranquil. This would have been about 9am. I was just positioning the vessel for offloading the equipment to the rig when this small canoe-type boat came close. On board were four local chaps dressed in their tribal gowns. All seemed fine.

The boat then moved around my vessel, as if the men were looking at certain items, then it moved around the drilling rig and seemed to go away.

I came close to the rig and commenced loading and offloading equipment, and all seemed to be going well. The armed soldiers on board were extremely observant and we maintained good communications with the rig as the offloading operation was being carried out.

Around 4pm, the same canoe-like boat came back. The people on board were no longer in tribal gowns but wearing army camouflage clothes. At the front of the boat was a person secured by a large belt in order to keep his balance, as, in his arms, he had a machine gun, which he started shooting! I immediately stopped our operation and started steaming away to a 'safe area', which was at least 30 metres away from the rig.

The small boat was following us, at a very good speed! Fortunately, with our stern wash (wake) the boat kept getting rolled about and was unable to keep steady, so the chase was aborted.

I kept running the vessel until we were at a very safe distance from the shoreline. I then called the rig and told them of my intentions. The 'company man' complained and said that I should return. I cannot repeat my response.

Such incidents went on for a few days and it was not good at all. I called my office in Switzerland and explained the situation to them. They could not fully grasp the danger but I must say that they supported me 100 per cent.

Eventually, the vessel completed the operations and, as this was a spot charter, when we arrived back to Port Harcourt, we were cleared out and moved well offshore. My job was as 'bunker barge' for our vessels, which meant that I was the offshore filling station for our company vessels. This operation was relatively safe, and I remained like this for another two weeks. Then my relief came out and I went home. I was very pleased to be leaving the area!

While I was on board the 'Red Swan', we got a visit from the incoming owner, the vice president of Seabulk Incorporated, who had come to give us some moral support. It was very good of him, as when we had a meeting with all the crew, he stated that we were doing a very good job etc. and that they were winning the competition. I did tell him that we were not winning the competition; the competitors were pulling out due to dangerous activities! So, it was just a matter of time before I left.

I stayed at home for my regular leave with my wife and family and enjoyed it very much. Then I received a call from my company to tell me to proceed to West Africa to Abidjan, on the Ivory Coast. This was around August 2001.

I had been there previously on a seismic vessel, so I joined the 'Seabulk Coot 1'; an anchor-handling/supply vessel. We would be tending a rig called the 'Ocean Liberator', which was drilling just about 30 miles away from Abidjan. This meant short and frequent trips to the dock and rig, which was tiresome! Also, a couple of times there were demonstrations or coups going on, but the French Government sent troops in to quell them, and they did a very good job.

We did a few runs with the rig and then the instruction was for the rig to go to Ghana, so we prepared for the tow and towed the rig to its new drilling site. Just before we sailed, we had a crew change. Some of the crew were Filipino and I knew them from the previous crew so, as always, welcomed them on board and we had our meetings.

We sailed from Abidjan (cleared out from customs and immigration) and to the rig.

I noticed that one of the new crew members did not look too good. He was the mechanic, and I asked him if he felt OK, and he replied, "Fine!" Normally, the crew members were all chirpy and swapping stories, but the mechanic did not get involved, so I was certainly going to watch him.

Once the Ghana project was complete, we had to tow the rig back to Abidjan for standby. The people on the rig were all ready to commence retrieving anchors, so we began. We had one of our sister ships, which was the 'Red Petrel', but she was having problems, so we tried to help and took as much of the work as we could.

We retrieved all the anchors and ourselves and 'Red Petrel' towed the rig back to Abidjan. However, the 'Red Petrel' was having steering problems, so we were unable to tow next to each other for safety reasons. We managed without any incidents, but it was uncomfortable to say the least.

When we were approaching Abidjan, the mechanic was still not too good. Throughout the trip, I was in constant contact with the medic from the rig, who was advising me. I was also in touch with our agent in Abidjan, giving him updates on the situation.

Near Abidjan, the agent organised for a small boat to come alongside. The mechanic was transferred and taken quickly ashore for medical attention.

It was about three days later, and we had completed positioning the rig and running anchors. We said our goodbyes to the rig and they thanked me tremendously for the work we had done, and then we sailed into the port of Abidjan. It felt good, as we were all getting ready to go home to our families.

When I got alongside, and things had quietened down, I just sat there on the bridge with a cup of tea, feeling good, as we had accomplished what everyone said we would not.

The agent came on board. He was a good chap and had done his job very well. When I saw that his face was ashen, I knew something was wrong. He said he was very sorry, but our mechanic had died in hospital. Prior to this, I had spoken to the agent about the condition of the mechanic, and he told me he was improving. To hear that he had died was terrible.

The agent said it was malaria, but a new strain, which he had picked up during his holiday. I felt really bad and wondered if any more crew members may have picked up malaria on their holidays?

The agent arranged for the remaining crew and me to visit the hospital for tests. We got the results back and there was the possibility that two or three crew members had been infected. Having been in colder climates, I was OK.

Eventually we disembarked and went home, feeling very sad.

'Seabulk Coot 1'.

I enjoyed my holiday with my wife and family very much. Then, I was called to go back to Abidjan, on the 'Seabulk Coot 1', which was in the shipyard. Maintenance was nearly finished, so she would be ready for the next contract. I asked where we were bound for and was told Luanda. I had been there before, and I was OK with that. So, I left home for Abidjan Ivory Coast.

I had been on board the 'Seabulk Coot 1' for a few days and we were preparing to sail, when all of a sudden, at the last moment, the plans were changed and I was scheduled to sail to Nigeria! Alarm bells were ringing and I knew I would not be going. I immediately told the office how I felt and the response was, "Things are quieter now," etc. Anyhow, I stood my ground and completely refused to sail the vessel. I told them to get another master to replace me, and they went on to say that there was no one available. Still, I stood my ground.

I was 'threatened' that I would never get another job with them again and so on. Again, I stood my ground! Eventually, a relief master arrived and took command, so I left for home.

227

I do not think I was at home for more than a week when the office asked me to go to Trinidad. That was quite a surprise for me. So away I went, to the 'Seabulk Grebe" the ex-'Smitloyd 120', which was a nice vessel.

The only problem was the vessel was in the dry dock at Trinidad with a broken propeller shaft, and the shipyard was not big enough to repair or replace the damaged one. Not only that, but the owner of the shipyard refused to release the vessel so that we could go to a more sophisticated shipyard, as he kept saying it was unsafe (maybe finances had a part to play?) It was not a nice time to join a vessel; you could say it was under shipyard arrest!

The owner of the shipyard was, of course, local, and all he wanted was our business, as he was getting a day rate. The truth was that he could not repair or replace our situation as he was not big enough, and each day was getting more stressful.

Eventually we sailed to a place called Curacao; a former Dutch colony in the Caribbean Sea. They were very professional and we got the repair done quite quickly, but prior to completion, I went home for days off. This was in June 2001.

After my days off, I was sent back to Trinidad and, again, assigned to the 'Seabulk Grebe' and also the 'Seabulk Cormorant', which was originally built for Maersk, but Care Offshore acquired it. It was not a bad vessel.

I spent the rest of my contract in Trinidad and, in view of Care Offshore, sold onto 'Seabulk'. I knew my time with the company was coming to an end and I would move on to new ventures.

'Seabulk Cormorant', (Captain Ken Shakesby).

Chapter 10

AROUND THE OIL FIELDS AND BACK

In December 2001, I'd had enough of moving from vessel to vessel, so decided to resign from the ships. (At a later date, I would wonder if this had been a mistake). I went home to rethink my future and, to be fair, I was in a quandary as to which way to go.

I got a message from a company called Matthews Daniel; an insurance company in London with bases around the world, including Egypt, where I had done some marine warranty work while on leave from the supply vessels. They put a proposition to me; a job as marine manager, be based in Cairo, Egypt, work three months on, one month off. I would have my own residence and other things. I took the job, but looking back, I think I jumped too quickly. But this is life.

I arrived at Cairo and was no stranger to the area, system, culture etc. so that was a positive start. My boss was a fellow Englishman called Mike Sanders. He also lived in Cairo, with his Egyptian wife, Mervat, and their son, Tim, who was about 12 years old.

I had to find comfortable accommodation in a nice area. While looking around, I stayed in a hotel, if I was not engaged in rig-moving duties offshore. I had a massive suitcase, as my length of stay was three months, so yes, it was somewhat uncomfortable. I would stay in the hotel, then, when I had to go offshore, I would take the amount of clothes I thought I'd need and leave my suitcase in the hotel.

Mervat advised me on finding an apartment that was 'value for money', as I was paid an allowance from the company for this. Mervat would take me 'house hunting'.

After many days, we finally found one I could see myself eventually living in. It was a three-bedroom flat on the third floor, with two balconies, and was very spacious. Mike did say to me that if I could wait, he would offer me first refusal on his accommodation (as he was getting his own place). I was not too impressed, though, as it was on the ground floor and I saw quite a lot of insects and cockroaches about. Once they came a-calling, it was very difficult to get rid of them, so I politely declined his offer and settled for the flat, which was adequate for me.

It took me a while to settle in and I bought certain things to make it more comfortable for me. I asked my wife her opinion and yes, she liked it, but she would not stay in the flat on her own and I certainly agreed with her decision. So if Jean visited and I had to go offshore, I would check her into the nearest hotel (5 star), then I knew she would be safe and relaxed.

For a time, we enjoyed the situation, as my family came to visit me, including some of my grandchildren, and they loved it. My wife invited her sisters and, of course, my job was to show them the Pyramids, Khan El Khalili Bazaar and lots of other interesting places.

When my wife was with me, it was good, and we enjoyed our time together in Egypt. Jean enjoyed meeting the people locals and ex-patriates.

When I started with Mat Dan (Matthews Daniel) it was hectic, as the office was not marine-minded and all the files and everything were in disarray. So when I got back to shore, I was up to my neck in it, getting things sorted as best I could.

I was settling in to my apartment and, of course, the people around me were local, as our office was in Heliopolis, Cairo, as opposed to the oil field city, downtown in Maadi, where nearly all the expats stayed.

I was happy with this set up as it was only a short distance to my office. Mainly, I was engaged in rig-moving with GlobalSantaFe and a local company. 50 per cent was owned by the Egyptian Government (hence EDC) and the other 50 per cent by the Danish company Maersk.

So the work was flowing. At this time, we had rigs working in the Gulf of Suez, which was south of the Suez Canal, but also up north in the Mediterranean Sea, so it was pretty constant, towing rigs through the Suez Canal. If the rigs were moving at the same time, we would contact a company in the UK, who would send some surveyors to help us out. They also got a decent day rate.

Eventually, I fell out with the owner of the UK company. As with other companies, he had his favourites and would only provide those people with jobs. I was not impressed. He was not my type of man; not to be trusted at any time. I used to think he was a decent chap, but that was a big mistake. Even now it leaves a bad taste in my mouth.

Anyway, onwards and upwards!

During my time with Mat Dan, I came across lots of nice people, whether they were local or expats. I was with Mat Dan for about five years as a marine manager in Egypt and yes, the job was hard, but there were times when I got back to shore and would have the weekend to myself, so would get my provisions in and give my apartment a good clean and then I could relax and be nice and quiet. Tranquillity at its best!

One year, there was to be a get-together of worldwide Mat Dan companies and the seminar/meeting would be held in Cairo. People in similar roles to ours would come and visit, so I could meet people I had something in common with, but who worked thousands of miles away from me.

Anyhow, our company meeting was getting close. Our office was in control and we had to make sure we put on a good show and welcomed our fellow work associates from around the world.

Mike, the office manager, was in charge of this project and, for sure, it took a lot of organising! It was to be held in Sharm El Sheik, south of Cairo and the Sinai. I called my wife and told her to come and that we would have a good time.

I lived very close to one of the hotels our people would be coming to, so the plan was for us to meet up in the hotel lounge on the day.

There were 14 people in total, which I know is not a lot, but it was an ideal amount. We had a drink in the hotel lounge and, as it was a six-hour drive, an air-conditioned bus with adequate provision of drinks and snacks (and seating up to 55 passengers) was our mode of transport.

We also had a plainclothes security guard travelling with us.

We got going at around 9am and all was good. My wife was sitting next to me, so I could not have wished for anything more.

We made quite a few stops on the way, at the usual roadside cafés, especially for the women, who were browsing, shopping and negotiating prices with the sellers.

We arrived in Sharm El Sheik around 3pm or so and everyone was looking forward to what was to come. We were staying at the Sheraton, which we knew was of a high standard.

The plan was to meet up again downstairs at a set time, so my wife and I unpacked our clothes and got everything ready for the evening. We had a 'power nap', which was much-appreciated.

We got ready for our dinner and went downstairs. The women were chatting among themselves, as were the men, then we got called for dinner. There was a really long table, outside on the grass, which had been very dressed up. The food was absolutely perfect; lobster and seafood, and the fine wines were really good.

In the morning, the company personnel attended the seminar, so the woman were free to have a look around the hotel and/or catch a little bit of sun. Everyone was really enjoying themselves.

One evening, we were invited to go and have our dinner in the desert in a Bedouin tent, which sounded very interesting!

We were driven to the area, which was only a few minutes away. Someone said to look up, and on the top of this a sand dune, someone had inserted wood coals. As they fired up, they spelt the words 'Mat Dan', so that was a nice sight!

We were served all kinds of food; it was really, really nice. Then the entertainment started, which were camel rides; also very interesting! Then we watched these young girls dressed in Arabic costumes belly dancing. They were so good and very artistic!

Eventually, the night came to an end and we were driven back to the hotel where we sat at the bar for a while and had drinks etc., then it was time for bed, after a very enjoyable day.

We attended the seminars each day, which were advancing our services to the industry. We had about four days in Sharm El Sheik, then returned to Cairo, and our work associates returned to their countries. We'd had a really good time and all got on well with each other.

I worked with the Egyptian people and had some really good friends and work associates. I still remember the good times.

One time, I was preparing for a rig move on a GlobalSantaFe rig called 'GSF Adriatic 4', which was in the Mediterranean Sea and was getting ready for moving. Out of the blue came a call from the GSF office. They needed me to travel ASAP to the Gulf of Suez, as one of their other rigs needed to move quickly. Of course, I got underway to the Gulf of Suez to a place called Abu Rhudeis. It was the 'GSF 105' and I got on board and prepared for the move.

It had worked out that my associates, Mohamed Baget and Haney Gamal, had gone onto the 'GSF Adriatic 4' and later on, the rig had a blow-out. Everything got out of control and gas was gushing to the surface etc. Of course, the rig was evacuated immediately and everyone took to the lifeboats. There was an explosion and it became a complete disaster.

All units in the vicinity were on standby assist; firefighting vessels and all types of offshore assistance were deployed. It took a long time for things to quieten down, as it was a massive field, supplying gas to Israel, Jordan and Syria. Eventually a further two drilling rigs arrived at a safe distance and they both drilled relief wells to take the pressure from the main blow-out area.

I boarded one of the relief units, which was the 'GSF Key Manhattan' and I was to observe the situation from the underwriter's perspective. Things were quietening down somewhat and progress was being made. Another unit was brought in from Maersk, which was about ten miles away, and I was in the jacking house of the 'GSF Key Manhattan', just observing things. I had a pair of binoculars and was watching the Maersk rig approaching the platform, with the tug boats positioning the rig.

It was daylight, nice weather, and there I was, observing, when all of a sudden, I saw the rig lurch towards the platform. I found out when I returned to the office that they'd had a punch-through, so really it was a disaster for the companies and all the people involved. Much devastation was caused, but thankfully no one lost their life.

So, for me, as a marine warranty surveyor, over a period of a few months, the situation with the Egyptian gas fields in the Mediterranean had been completely devastating for the government and owners.

Sometime later, during a GSF rig-moving operation, I was approached and asked if I would be interested in working for GSF. I said, "Yes, I am always interested in furthering my career."

The marine managers were quite friendly and would attend the rig moves sometimes. One of them asked me if I would like a job as barge master, which would be based in Egypt. I'd work 28 days on and 28 off, which suited me down to the ground.

So again, I was moving into new areas and challenges.

I was at home when I got a call from GSF to travel to Aberdeen for an interview for my new work role as barge master. When I arrived, it was somewhat surprising, as the people who were supposed to interview me were very apprehensive and told me they felt out of their depths interviewing me!

The interview finished and all was fine. I started to head off home, due to join the rig 'GSF Adriatic 10' in the middle of January. It was December, so I thought that was good. I asked when my pay started and they said, "Not until you get to the rig!" I said, "That is nearly a month away. I will not go a month without any salary, so forget the interview and I will look elsewhere for work." Of course, they were surprised by my comments and after a few phone calls, I got put on pay and would join the rig in the first week of January 2005, which was fine with me.

So I went home and enjoyed my Christmas with my wife and family.

I was sent out to the drilling rig 'GSF Adriatic 10', which was drilling in the Mediterranean Sea and crew-changing from Port Said, Egypt. I already knew quite a few of the crew as they had been on board certain rigs when I had been engaged as MWS (marine warranty surveyor) so at least that was to my advantage. There were also expats on board, whom I got to know, and they were decent people, so in general, things were good.

In the first 12 months, each time I went on leave, I had to do some kind of course. I got my Class 1 barge master licence within the company and also the Flag administration of offshore installation manager, in case (God forbid) there were any emergences and the OIM needed me to take over. I was doing firefighting courses, sometimes in Egypt, other times in the UK, and I covered lots of rig offshore courses. I even passed my supervisor's well control course for drilling, even though the barge master position was of marine background. The strangest request was that I do my 'rig movers' course, which involved six assessed rig moves. This had been my role, prior to becoming a barge master, so it was strange. The company management did not know which direction to take as they knew I had been on numerous rig-moves, so the management agreed I would do just one assessed move. So then, the underwriter sent an MWS for the rig move, and also to assess me, but the sad thing is that no one would come to assess me, as I was the one who assessed them! So yes, it was strange. Eventually, an MWS did turn up and it was one of the chaps I had trained! He felt uncomfortable about the situation, but I put him at ease and told him not to worry.

The rig move was carried out in a professional manner and all went well. I obtained my certification from the underwriter and my company, GlobalSantaFe.

So all was going well and I stayed on the drilling rig 'GSF Adriatic X' as barge master/rig mover.

After one year, there were changes made within the company and I was transferred to one of the sister rigs close by, which was the 'GSF Key Singapore'.

I got on board and all was good, as, again, I knew lots of people, especially the local crew, as well as third parties who came to the rig for drilling programmes. The OIM (offshore installation manager) was a nice chap whom I had known from doing rig moves.

The year was 2007 and I got a call from my wife. There had been a big storm in my town and everywhere was flooded. I was close to my departure time and when I got home, my wife met me at the airport. She told me that the insurance company had put her into a hotel whilst the damage to our house was assessed.

237

On the Saturday, I left my wife in the hotel, as she was too upset to see the condition the house was in. I met with the insurance surveyor and was told by the neighbours that a river of water had run in the direction of our house, and while all the pumps underground were pumping the water to the local reservoir, the reservoir then burst its banks and the water was full of bacteria etc. When I looked around our house, the water had drained away by then, but I just cried. It had filled up the bottom half of our house to a height of more than 1.5 metres. It was absolutely disgusting, and everything was ruined.

So my wife and I had to stay in the hotel until we found temporary residence. They estimated at least six months before we could get back in the house. My wife and I were absolutely devastated.

We found a small flat above a shop in nearby Willerby, and it was nine months before we got back into our house. Life is so strange isn't it?

A few weeks had gone by and my wife and I were in bed, at around midnight. I must have dozed off, when all of a sudden, I woke up, and what I saw and felt was totally weird and frightening.

The bedroom walls were going up and down, in and out! My wife was crying, and it really was frightening. I had never experienced anything like it in my life! It finished as quickly as it had started. The first thing I thought, when everything had stopped, was that someone must be in the house (maybe just a man thing!) I got dressed and ran into the other bedrooms; nothing. So I dashed downstairs and had a look around; nothing there. I opened the front door and went into the street. My neighbour said, "Switch on the television."

So I did, and the latest news flash was on. Then I understood. . . what we had experienced was an earthquake! The epicentre was just 30 miles away! At least I knew what it was. I then comforted my wife, explaining it to her, and we managed to go back to bed and to sleep.

The following day, I climbed into our loft to see if we had received any cracks to the structure, but all was fine. What a night that had turned out to be.

I stayed on the 'GSF Key Singapore' for quite some time, during periods of excitement; for example, the 'GSF Adriatic 4' sinking. Well, now the oil company decided to move another drilling rig over the now wasted platform to finally 'kill' all the remaining wells, so I was appointed to move our rig to that position. We had an ROV (remote operated vehicle) which would show us how the 'GSF Adriatic 4' was laying and how close it was to the platform. I managed to manoeuvre our rig into a safe position, within 20 feet, which was pretty close. All was good, then a team of Americans came on board called 'Wild West', who were experts in 'killing off' wells.

Needless to say, we stayed in that position for over a year, making the area safe so that there would be no more blow-outs in that area.

Eventually, we completed the job and moved to another location to commence drilling operations. I must say that at this time I was getting emails from a company in Aberdeen, asking if I would work for them, but at that time, the name on the email was not familiar to me, so I kind of let it go over my head.

During these times, the company GlobalSantaFe was being taken over by a company called Transocean, which was a very big company. In Egypt, there was a slow campaign onshore of changing out the GSF's employees with Transocean, especially at management level. Transocean had an award called the 'first excellence award', which was given to the rig which worked the most safely and, of course, the 'GSF Key Singapore' had won it this particular time. They needed a rig employee to go to Houston, USA, to receive the award, and guess who was nominated? Yes, it was me! At the time, I was on leave, but the company told me all about it and I was pleased to have been chosen.

They told me my wife could go with me, which was really good! So we started to prepare for the event.

The area manager called me at home and said I could go anytime, so we decided to go five days prior to the event. The company flew us business class on a special chartered plane and had booked out hotel. Everything was taken care of! It was a nice flight and of course, on our arrival, we were greeted and shown to our hotel, which was so nice.

We got settled in, relaxed and acclimatised.

The next day, I called our Houston office to see if they could recommend a reliable taxi driver so that my wife and I could go and do some sightseeing. The company straight away told us there was a driver on standby!

We visited quite a few places, including Galveston and Temah Gardens. We were having a really nice time! Also, we had people from our division, along with their wives, so it was good for my wife as she had some female company. There were also people from the same company, but worldwide, so it was good to mingle with the other people.

We met with the CEO at that time, who was a decent chap.

Of course, I went onto the stage to collect my award and made a small speech. I was a little bit out of my comfort zone, but I managed, and the presentation was complete! Then everyone was more relaxed. It was really good and enjoyable.

We stayed there for about nine days in total, then it was time to head back home, and by this time, my holiday was coming to an end.

We decided that once we landed in Amsterdam, I would continue to Egypt and my wife would take the short flight alone, back to the UK. Jean was fine with that, as she had travelled on her own overseas many times and was very confident. The company were grateful to me for doing this, as it meant that the rig's other barge master could leave the rig on time for his holiday.

At this time, around August 2008, I had arrived back in Cairo to catch the helicopter to the rig. At the heliport, I saw a group of managers. With it being my first day, I kept a low profile. I saw the HSE manager, area manager and also some others, so I decided to see why they were going to our rig. It seemed as if there had been an accident, but nothing life-threatening.

We landed on the rig and I did my handover. They all left and then I found out that the people coming on with me were an investigation team, as one of the local drillers had slipped on the floor of the rig and twisted his ankle. It could have been 10 times worse. Anyhow, they did their investigation and before departing, they had had a meeting with the rig management. Bearing in mind I was not on the rig when it happened ,so there was nothing I could add, I was told to be present at the meeting.

The area manager went on and on! He said that the supervision on the rig was unacceptable etc. By this time, I was getting more and more angry. I was sitting next to my OIM, who nudged me and said to keep quiet! So, after this, the manager finished his disgusting speech about the rig supervisors and asked, "Any questions?" No one answered, so I said, "Excuse me, but I have not long ago been across to Houston to receive the 'first excellence award' for safety, so that must mean something?" He looked at me with contempt and said, "That is history!" I told the area manager I had arrived just that day after my holiday and asked him to accept my resignation. I was so angry with him! He replied, "Is it because of the criticism I have just give you?" My answer was, "Mister, I have much bigger problems than you have!" He was not a happy bunny.

So they left the rig and we picked ourselves up and got stuck in for the next 28 days.

When the time came for me to go home, the OIM called me on my office phone and told me my relief would be late, so I said "And?" He said, "Company policy: no relief, no go!" I then stated that I had given notice of my resignation 28 days previously, so was off regardless.

I told the OIM to ring at the same time tomorrow, as it surely wouldn't be me answering!

Needless to say, I left the rig and arrived at my house the following morning, around 9:30am. I explained to my wife what had happened etc. I opened up my emails and there was one from the company CEO, saying 'Ken, what the f**k is going on?' At that time, I was tired from travelling, so I said, 'Forget it, Bob'. I really should have told him exactly what had happened and asked for a transfer to another area, but it went out of my mind. I never contacted the company again, even though people asked me to come back. I would not accept being spoken to by management as if I was dirt.

So, it seemed as if my career had come to another turning point! The truth was that I had nothing to go to.

I mentioned earlier that I had been receiving emails from a company in Aberdeen, called Trident Offshore. I called them and they arranged a flight to Aberdeen. I arrived at the company address and presented myself to the lady at the desk. I immediately asked her if she was sure she had the right man (me) as my son was also in the oil and gas industry. Immediately, there was a voice behind me saying, "Yes, we have the right man."

I looked round and it was Dennis Pedersen. I knew him from way back, when I was an MWS in Egypt and he had come on the rig move for Maersk as a trainee tow master. He then told me had left Maersk and come to this company as marine manager. He asked me if I would work with them as a field marine supervisor, as staff. Anyhow, we had a talk and at that time, it seemed appealing.

Of course, it meant that I would be offshore quite a lot, as tow master/marine representative etc. but the good thing was that I could work from home. That seemed fine and I agreed.

Quite a few times I asked myself the question, "Have I done the right thing?" and often I wondered if I had made a mistake. I was receiving a monthly income and would go out into the field with other team members. If we were sent abroad, I found out that the contractors (who were doing the same job I was) would get an extra bonus, because of environmental issues! As staff, I was just getting a basic rate, which I was not very pleased with! During this time, the marine manager, Dennis, had resigned and moved on, and of course another chap took his place. I kindly told him that I should get the environmental allowance, as the other team members did, and he was coming up with all sorts of excuses so that he would not have to pay me. At the end of the conversation, he suggested it had been an agreement between the previous manager and the team, which I told him was ridiculous! Eventually he backed down and said he would give it to me this time, but not again. So alarm bells were ringing.

By this time, the company had been changed from Trident Offshore to Intermoor (part of the Acteon Group).

Anyhow, I worked in the North Sea, across to Europe, Black Sea, Egypt, India, China, Trinidad, Falklands, so I did get around.

When we went to India to do a rig move, we travelled to a place called Kakanada, and it was the first time I had been, so I thought it would be interesting. We arrived at the local airport after changing at Mumbai and were met by officials, then transported to the dockside office, where we met with the client. At that time, the weather was about 40°C, so you can imagine how uncomfortable it was! When the meeting was complete, we were told that they would take us to our accommodation (bearing in mind, on the way there, we had seen nothing that looked like a hotel). We were scheduled to sail out to the rig the following day.

Well, we came to this small village and there were cows, goats, sheep, dogs, just strolling about! I thought, "Where are they taking us?"

We arrived at this small building which looked fairly new. We were taken inside and what a pleasant surprise I had, as there were three floors, and on each floor were three rooms, a kitchen and a lounge! More importantly, the air conditioning was on and it was so cool! Excellent.

We each picked a room and I saw, through the false wardrobe door, there was a WC and shower room. We got changed into more relaxed clothes and quickly showered. All was good! We then went downstairs to the 'main' kitchen. There was a team of catering staff waiting for us, who told us they would be available 24/7, but that was not needed.

I had my meal and a brief chat with the team, then went to bed and had a great sleep. I

woke up to the sound of barking dogs and crowing birds, but I did not mind.

So, up, dressed, breakfasted and down to our transport at the dock to take us to the rig, 'Essar Wildcat.' We did the move (uneventful) and then all returned to the UK until the next project came up.

The time came and I went to China for rig move operations. Richard Holt and I were both tow masters and we had a couple of chaps from our mooring chain department, as one of our jobs was to change out the rig's anchoring system. So there were six team members from the UK.

When we arrived in Hong Kong, we met up with three other work associates from Intermoor, USA.

We had to travel back and forth between Hong Kong and China for visas etc. as we needed resident status to enable us to do the work. We eventually received a permit to enter China and, when we arrived, we had to go through certain administration tasks etc. which was not a problem. Then we had medicals and, I must say, everything was professional, no waiting etc.

It was at this time, during a scan, that the nurse told me she could only detect one kidney! I was a little taken aback and thought she had got it wrong, but she, of course, was completely correct! It was strange, finding out after all those years that I only had one kidney! None of the medicals I'd had in the UK had picked up on it! I wondered if my incident with the winch on the 'Dunsley Wyke' back in the late 1960s had had something to do with it.

When we were all sorted out with the permits etc., we went to the dockyard to board the semi-submersible rig, 'Nanhai V'. At first, I felt that the welcome was a very nervous one, as I believe it was the first time Europeans had done the rig-moving operation. We eventually won their trust and things became more comfortable.

Prior to boarding the rig, I got myself a knife and fork from the hotel, and that was the best thing I ever did, as I couldn't manage the chopsticks! The food, I must admit, was not the best, but I managed, and yes, the Chinese crew were really good people. This particular operation went smoothly and we got the rig in its intended position, so all parties were happy.

During my period with Intermoor, I did return to Egypt for rig-moving. I was asked if I would be interested in the position of manager, based onshore. This would involve meeting clients etc. I said I would be interested, so one time, they sent me out to look for accommodation for my wife and myself. At this time, there was already a base man onshore, so I started looking around with our company's agent.

The place Aberdeen Intermoor Management chose was good, but when I found out (there were a lot of things I did not know about) what their intentions were, I was not impressed! Anyhow, I knew that the present base manager wanted to go back home to the UK for a few days, but I kept quiet, and when the shouting quietened down about my new prospects and working in Egypt, the company said, "OK, Ken, never mind about the potential job offer; will you stay in Egypt for a week to manage the onshore business?"

I was so angry at the way they had messed me and my family about that I immediately said no, and that I would be on the flight to the UK first thing in the morning. The company was certainly not happy with my response and yes, I did depart Egypt the following morning and return to the UK.

Later on, I had communications with the operations manager of the Aberdeen office. I really let loose with my feelings! He tried to back-pedal out of the situation. So, in general, to say I was disappointed with the way I had been treated was an understatement. I was furious! I handed in my resignation and left within 28 days.

Much to my surprise, a few months later, I got a message from the operations manager, who told me, eventually, that he too had resigned, due to higher management. Also, the way I had been treated influenced his decision to resign. For me, the company had just been disgusting with the way they treated personnel.

There were lots of things, I did not agree with. I was what was called 'office staff' and when a team of us were deployed to a foreign country, we had to pay with our private accounts, which I was not impressed with! One time, one of the team didn't have a bank card, so the rest of the team had to finance him until we got back home! I approached one of the operations managers and asked him if I could have a company card, and his response was, "I will have to check with head office." Well, that said it all for me, as if the operations team had to request something like that, I was going nowhere with the company. So, in disgust, I just told him to forget it, as he had no authority whatsoever. To say the least, he was not too pleased with my remark.

Most of the people were good, it was just the odd few in higher management that were full of their own importance. Plus there was a little clique, which I was not too happy about, but that is life. The job I was engaged in and the way the system worked were not for me, but now I was at an age where I was getting somewhat concerned, as it felt like I could be stuck in a trap.

So, I decided to escape and go on another journey. This would have been around 2007. I knew that Intermoor was not going to be the last company I worked for. I did work with them until 2012, then I thought the grass could be greener on the other side.

I sat down with my wife and we discussed our future. Would I retire, or would I continue to work, even if it meant slowing down some? By now, we had seven grandchildren and three great-grandchildren!

It was May 2017. As I've mentioned, my wife was also from a fisherman's family, and I must put this section in my book, as my wife really deserves it. Jean was engaged in a local play called 'Lil's Lassies', which was about a Hull lady called Lillian Bilocca. This lady spearheaded the determination of the Hull trawlermen's wives to achieve a safer working environment for their husbands, partners, families and friends. What Lillian started changed the future of Hull's deep-sea trawlermen. So, a local play was put on as Hull's thank you to this wonderful woman.

My wife had been asked to take part in this play, as she was one of the original women who had marched silently back in 1968, when we had the Hull triple trawler tragedy. At that time, Jean was 19 years old; a young wife and mother, and very supportive of me.

When the time came for rehearsals, my wife was very nervous, as she had never done anything like this in her life! I supported her to the best of my ability and was extremely proud of her throughout.

There were five performances, presented to full audiences each evening. I was, and still am, so very proud of my wife, and the acting brought back so many memories. I still have tears in my eyes, it felt so real.

While the play was in rehearsal, my wife had an interview with a reporter from Look North; the local BBC news programme. At the memorial site for the lost Hull fishermen, Jean talked to the reporter about the play and her late father, who was lost overboard back in 1963. It was so touching.

My wonderful, darling wife was asked to do a repeat of the play in November 2017. She was really looking forward to it, and so was I! Again, it ran for five nights; again, to packed audiences!

Then Jean said she had pain in her side, so I took her to the Hull Royal Infirmary, where she was seen by a doctor. It was late evening. The chap who saw her said it was nothing to worry about etc and prescribed painkillers. So we went home.

The next day, I took Jean back to the hospital, as she was still in pain. Again, she was seen, and then they did an X-ray and said that her bowels were compacted. I felt unsure and very insecure about the way we were being told things. My wife then had an ultrasound, and the man who did the scan blew our world apart when he said she had cancer.

We got a letter through the post, asking Jean to go to the Castle Hill hospital to see a specialist. They did these checks and told us, "Go home and pack some things for a stay in the hospital." You can imagine how we felt already, and then they give us that blow! They said my wife needed tests.

We also visited our GP, who sat there, looked into my wife's face and said, "I am sorry to say this, Mrs Shakesby, but you have got bowel and kidney cancer." Well, I sat there, deep in shock, and my wife, God bless her, was lost for words. I was asking questions and I knew I was losing the plot with this so-called GP.

Jean and I went home and told our children.

We went to the hospital and they carried out the tests. I felt that the different specialists who visited my wife at her bedside were saying things contrary to each other, so, as a family were completely dumbfounded.

I stayed for as long as I could with my wife and made sure there was a member of the family with her at all times. They kept her in for a few days whilst carrying out the tests. One specialist said, "Yes, we will keep your wife here in the hospital" and the next one said, "She can go home"! I felt as if no one was taking responsibility.

My wife did get discharged and I brought her home. She was still in pain, so I called the ward and they said to bring her back. Jean had further tests and then, after a few days, this was the outcome: "We have misdiagnosed your wife and she does *not* have any kidney or bowel problems." Can you believe that? I was initially in shock and so overcome with relief! I was trying to come to terms with what the incompetence of the NHS had put my wife through.

We went home and, again, went to see our GP. I cannot tell you how I felt, but we were talking about my wife's liver and wanted a referral from the GP to go private. However, the GP said there was no need as her blood tests were good etc.

So, we took his advice. This was the month of January 2018. Then, some months later, my wife had to see a specialist again. He told her that there was a problem with her liver. Now they say that my wife has cirrhosis of the liver which, of course, is life-threatening.

We are trying to get through these difficult times. My wife was featured in a documentary on BBC 3 about Hull's trawlers and the lives of the fishermen and their families. She was excellent, and I am so, so proud of her.

I was also in the documentary, as I was spare hand on the 'Kingston Garnet' when the 'Ross Cleveland' went down.

I remember the lights flickering in the storm, then eventually disappearing. I was 20 years old and I was just in shock. Everything was totally blank. So I'll come back to my wife's play and say that when the ladies to re-enacted this, it really took guts to see it through.

Now we are, in the present. Yes, these recent months have been a roller coaster. There have been some good times and some bad times. My wife is managing her illness with dignity and she will not give in to it. I admire and love her so much for this. We hope to have a quiet, healthy period from now on, as we are past our retiring ages. Hopefully I will be able to sit in my chair, read my memoirs and relive my memories of all the fishermen and others I met and worked with throughout my career, and think about the people I won't see again.

It must be true, what they say. . . that you cannot put an old sea dog down, as I still manage to come offshore and get involved with the rig move operations in the oil and gas division. I must admit that the phone keeps ringing and I keep going! I seem to be so lucky, as my time offshore is not too long and, 90 per cent of the time, I have good communications with my wife and we are doing OK.

Jean, God bless her, still gets invited to schools and the children are so interested in the Hull's deep-sea trawling industry. I feel good that all the lost souls and bereaved families will never be forgotten, and I am sure that the younger generations will remember Hull when it was the biggest fishing port in the United Kingdom.

I hope you have been able to visualise yourself in the situations I was placed in, good and bad.

I am now coming to the end of my memoirs and yes, I think I would do it all over again!

ABOUT THE AUTHOR

Born in Hull in 1947, down Eastbourne Street, off Hessle Road, Ken Shakesby knew from an early age that he would spend his working life as a trawlerman; inspired and influenced by his father, who was a Hull trawlerman.

Hessle Road had a thriving community, inextricably linked to the Hull deep-sea fishing fleets. Father and son were destined to work aboard these vessels.

Having attended the Boulevard High School from the age of 11, the 'normal' career path for young men was to 'go to sea'.

In 1960, at the tender age of 13, Ken Shakesby stowed away for three weeks to Iceland, on board a Hull trawler named 'Lord Essendon'; much to the horrifying surprise of his parents.

This gave Ken a flavour for the excitement and adventure that being a trawlerman offered, and so he left school in the year of 1962, taking up rank as galley boy on board another trawler, 'Stella Polaris'.

It wasn't all plain sailing, though Ken enjoyed his career path for the most part; not least the excitement and anticipation when 'hauling' the nets to see the bounty within.

However, these exciting times soon changed to dark periods, with Ken experiencing the 'Cod Wars', treacherous sea conditions and terrifying near-misses.

Ken battled through and vowed to carry on in an industry that, at that time, had scant regard for safety and demonstrated a culture of greed, as shown by the vessel owners.

In 1975, Ken's hard work paid off when he achieved the highest rank possible; that of skipper.

Ken's is a story of naivety, overcoming adversity in the face of fear, profound sadness at the loss of many friends and associates, the happiness of family life, along with the struggles of living a life at sea and the incessant desire to be at home with his family.

Lightning Source UK Ltd.
Milton Keynes UK
UKHW020726210119
335921UK00008B/45/P